QUIET TIMES WITH THE ONE YOU LOVE

A Devotional Guide for Couples

ART HUNT

Multnomah Publishers *Sisters, Oregon*

QUIET TIMES WITH THE ONE YOU LOVE
published by Multnomah Publishers, Inc.

© 1998 by Art Hunt

International Standard Book Number: 1-57673-257-6

Printed in the United States of America

Cover photo by Stewart Cohen/Tony Stone Images

Unless otherwise indicated, Scripture quotations are from:
The Holy Bible, New International Version (NIV)
© 1973, 1984 by International Bible Society,
used by permission of Zondervan Publishing House

Also quoted:
New American Standard Bible (NASB)
© 1960, 1977 by the Lockman Foundation

The New Testament in Modern English, Revised Edition (Phillips)
© 1972 by J. B. Phillips

The Good News Bible: The Bible in Today's English Version (TEV)
© 1976 by American Bible Society

The New English Bible (NEB) © 1976 by Oxford University Press

The Amplified Bible © 1965 by Zondervan Publishing House

The Message © 1993 by Eugene H. Peterson

For information:
MULTNOMAH PUBLISHERS, INC.•POST OFFICE BOX 1720•SISTERS, OREGON 97759

98 99 00 01 02 03 04 05 — 10 9 8 7 6 5 4 3 2 1

This book is affectionately dedicated to the couples of
Lighthouse Christian Center
in Puyallup, Washington.

ACKNOWLEDGMENTS

My sincere thanks and appreciation to:

Dan Benson—Your wisdom, insight, direction, and listening ear supplied just what I needed when I needed it.

Lisa Lauffer and Candace McMahan—Your editing skills and Christlike concern made all the difference.

The rest of the Multnomah team—You make writing a pleasure!

Dave Boyer—Your friendship and prayer support mean a great deal to me.

The Leadership Committee of Lighthouse Christian Center—I appreciate so much your generous hearts.

And most warmly, thank you, Naomi—This book was your idea in the first place. What a good gift you are to me!

Contents

HOW TO GROW YOUR SPIRITUAL FRIENDSHIP

Have you been looking for a way to spiritually enrich your marriage? Then this book is for you! I've written *Quiet Times with the One You Love* with one objective in mind: to help you and your spouse grow closer as spiritual friends. As you deepen your spiritual intimacy with each other, you'll find your marriage flooded with new warmth, vitality, and joy.

How important is the spiritual dimension of your marriage? Author James Dobson once received a letter that stands as an eloquent reminder of the importance of spirituality in marriage. Listen to this woman's letter:

> My husband recently left me after fifteen years of marriage. We had a great physical, emotional, and intellectual relationship. But something was missing...we had no spiritual bond between us. Please tell young couples that...a good marriage must have its foundation in Him in order to experience lasting love, peace, and joy.[1]

If barriers exist in your spirituality as a couple, your relationship is affected just as much or more as if you had other barriers between you. Relational distance is the inevitable result of failure to come together spiritually. On the other hand, couples who develop the spiritual dimension of their marriages virtually guarantee closer marital bonds.

What Is Spiritual Friendship?

When you examine the lives of spiritually intimate couples, you find two elements active in their spiritual friendship: (1) They develop a relationship with God *as a couple,* participating together in activities such as prayer, Bible reading, and devotions; and (2) they share their *individual* spiritual lives with each other, discussing their beliefs and sharing new insights gained from their times alone with the Lord.

As marriage partners develop spiritual intimacy, they experience a gradual lowering of relational barriers. They learn to overcome their sense of discomfort as they share their spiritual lives with each other. As this spiritual friendship begins to thrive, the couple often experiences more open communication and emotional safety. The result of developing spiritual friendship is that walls come down between husband and wife and between the couple and their Father. What could be more satisfying, more significant, or more challenging?

How This Book Can Help You
Deepen Your Spiritual Friendship

To help you develop your spiritual friendship, I've included in this book the basic elements for a quiet time together. A quiet time can be as brief or as long as you like, depending on how much time you need for Bible reading, prayer, and spiritual conversation. Each of the devotions in this book provides a Bible passage and comments about how to apply that passage to your life and marriage. Each devotion also includes a section called "Reflections," a set of questions that help you apply the day's Bible passage and devotional comments to your lives. Finally, the "Prayer Focus" in each devotion can guide you in praying specifically about what you've read and discussed.

The Value of Spiritual Conversation

Couples who successfully develop their spiritual friendship do so by sharing their spiritual journeys with each other. The "Reflections" at the end of each devotion will offer wonderful opportunities for you to foster this part of your relationship. This back and forth sharing of your spiritual journeys cannot help but strengthen every other facet of your marriage relationship.

Many of the devotions included in this book offer insight specifically about marriage and family issues. You may notice, however, that some devotions tap into subjects that aren't directly related to your marriage. I purposely included such variety. I believe that each devotion, whether specifically about marriage or not, can enhance your relationship because discussing and praying about a diversity of issues helps ensure a shared spiritual bond.

The Value of Couple Prayer

Couple prayer floods a marriage with the warm glow of God's presence. Praying together contributes something unique to your relationship and deepens your love for God and for each other. Through the "Prayer Focus" section of each devotion, you have an opportunity to experience these benefits.

One of the primary benefits of praying together is developing couple intimacy. Relational intimacy has to do with each spouse's willingness to reveal who he or she is and, in turn, understand and accept the other for doing the same. When two people pray together, truly seeking God as a couple, they reveal who they are to God *and* to each other. When I hear my wife pray, "Father, I'm concerned about my schedule next week" or "Lord, I want to love You more," she reveals herself to me, and I know her better. When couples pray together week after week, year in and year out, they understand each other's hearts. They cannot help but grow closer to each other.

Ready, Set, Go!

Quiet Times with the One You Love combines Bible reading, prayer, and spiritual conversation in a way that will help grow your spiritual friendship. This book contains 120 devotions, enough selections to last well over a year if you do two devotions each week. Each devotion may take as little as ten minutes or as long as an hour, according to your needs and desires. If you want to make your quiet times with each other longer than ten minutes, simply take more time for spiritual discussion and couple prayer.

If you're ready to deepen your spiritual friendship, if you're set to see some exciting things happen in your relationship as a result, then *Quiet Times with the One You Love* is for you. Enjoy your times together with your spouse and with your Lord.

1

BECOMING PRAYER PARTNERS

Husbands, in the same way be considerate as you live with your wives,
and treat them with respect...so that nothing will hinder your prayers.

1 PETER 3:7

I want to ask you a personal question. Do you pray together? I know you probably say grace at meals and pray on special occasions, but do you have a meaningful prayer life together?

You might be surprised to learn that according to my research—both formal and informal—many Christian couples aren't prayer partners.

If you aren't praying together regularly, please don't feel guilty and think, *Oh, no...one more thing we're not doing right.* I would, however, like to stir your thinking in this area. According to 1 Peter 3:7, it's important to properly maintain your marital relationship so that your prayer union won't be disturbed. Essentially the verse says, "Couples, maintain your relationship with each other so that you can also maintain your relationship with God." This passage clearly implies that couples should pray together, pursuing friendship with God *as couples.*

In over twenty years of marriage, praying with my wife, Naomi, has been a powerful, positive force in our relationship, simultaneously drawing us closer to God and to each other. I remember praying with Naomi early in our marriage and hearing her pour out her heart to God. As I listened, I thought, *She trusts me.* She was being real with God—talking about her feelings and needs—right in front of me. Couple prayer promotes intimacy; over time, marriage partners progressively reveal who they are to each other as well as to God.

Sometimes couples don't pray together because they feel too vulnerable. Men, especially, have difficulty in this area. One husband told me he was a loner when he first married his wife. About five years into their marriage, his wife asked if he would pray with her. He didn't want to but just couldn't say no. Twenty-five years later, he told me this: "The thing that has made the greatest difference in our lives as a couple has been my willingness to be vulnerable with her through prayer."

If you haven't tried praying together, discuss the reasons with each other. Partners can overcome the stumbling blocks to couple prayer if they simply talk about these obstacles, revealing their fears, sharing their hopes, and choosing to make some changes. The how-to's of couple prayer can be discovered in God's Word and, if you need more information, in many fine books. Simply start small and progress from there.

Come on, isn't it about time you discovered the joys and benefits of praying with the one you love?

REFLECTIONS: If you already pray together, share with each other what your prayer relationship means to you. If you don't pray together, identify the major obstacle(s) to doing so. Is the problem time? fear of intimacy? conflict? the fact that neither of you takes responsibility? What can you do to develop as prayer partners?

PRAYER FOCUS: If you are just beginning as prayer partners, pray for five minutes together. Start with thanksgiving and praise, continue by praying for others' needs, then pray for your own needs. End the same way you began—with thanksgiving and praise.

2
GOD ALLOWS U-TURNS

What I have vowed I will make good.

JONAH 2:9

When you married, did you have someone videotape or audiotape your wedding ceremony? If so, have you replayed that tape recently? Next time you do, pause for a moment and consider your marriage vows, those wild promises you made to the one you love. If you're like most, you said you would love, honor, and cherish. Precious words.

I clearly remember the vows I made before God to my bride: to love her no matter the price, to honor her in every circumstance, to cherish her no matter how difficult. Once in a while I ask myself the question, "How am I doing?"

Why don't you ask yourselves the same question today? How are you doing at fulfilling the vows you made to each other? Are you "making good" on your promise? Or are you having difficulty in one area or another?

The book of Jonah may offer you some help. "What," you may ask, "does the story of Jonah have to do with marriage vows?" Listen to Jonah's prayer from inside a whale's belly: "What I have vowed I will make good."

You know the story. Jonah was fleeing from God, destination Tarshish, but with a little help from his Father, he decided to make a U-turn. These eight words announce his change of heart. Certainly his was a desperate prayer, an anguished prayer, but it was also a repentant prayer. Jonah decided that he would make good what he had vowed.

God always allows us the option of going our own way in life; Jonah certainly exercised that option. He ran from God full speed ahead, flexing that volitional muscle we call "free will."

Why could Jonah resist God? Well, our heavenly Father could have made us like robots: Push a button and out comes "I love you." He could have made us like toy soldiers: Wind us up and away we go to do God's bidding. Instead, He made each of us with a heart, a spirit, a will. We can choose to say yes or no to His directives. We can embrace our Father's will or we can travel in the opposite direction.

Certainly that applies to our marriage promises as well. Sometimes married couples pursue a direction that is the opposite of God's desires: a hard knot of sustained anger, a heart too stubborn to admit wrong, a refusal to forgive, a conflict allowed to fester. God wants you to make that U-turn, to move back in His direction. Make good the vows you made before your Father to love boldly, to honor fully, to cherish wholly.

If you're headed in the wrong direction, turn around. Admit wrong; pursue the right. Put Tarshish in your rearview mirror! Find a fresh start with God and with each other.

REFLECTIONS: Can you identify an area of your relationship in which you're having trouble fulfilling your marriage vows? If so, what would a U-turn entail for you?

PRAYER FOCUS: Pray for courage to make good your marriage vows, for strength to pursue God's direction, for humility to receive His grace, and for joy in the process.

3
LEARNING TO LISTEN

He who answers before listening—that is his folly and his shame.
PROVERBS 18:13

Most spouses know the importance of listening to each other. Important, and oh so difficult! Maybe you've experienced a time or two when your listening abilities were less than exemplary.

Ask my wife, and she'll tell you that I'm normally a good listener; after all, I've been teaching couples to listen for years! But she'll also tell you I slip up now and then. Let me tell you about a situation when I blew it big time.

I had just come home from a leadership conference with a great new idea for the church that I pastor. I was excited about it; I just knew it would be exactly what we needed. When I described this great idea to Naomi, she frowned and shook her head. She didn't think it was a good idea.

I usually ask my wife to share her impressions with me so I can understand her objections. But this time I did something that blew the conversation wide open. I said to her, "Naomi, I'm immune to that frown. I know that this is the right way to go." Stupid, I know, but I felt so passionate about that idea!

My wife and I are both even-tempered, so we didn't yell at each other, but our listening skills went out the window. (And we lead marriage-enrichment seminars!) We were trying to convince each other of our positions. Both of us walked away hurt from the interaction.

A few minutes later we talked again. I said, "Honey, this thing was all my fault. I was wrong not to listen carefully to you. If I had listened to you at the beginning instead of trying to convince you, I know you would have listened to me, too. Can we start over?"

She forgave me. We then had a wonderful conversation that drew us closer together and opened our eyes to each other's point of view. If I had just listened carefully in the first place, I could have avoided some of the pain.

Proverbs 18:13 is right: When you talk without listening, all kinds of problems arise. After working with hundreds of couples, I'm convinced that one of the greatest gifts you can give your spouse is the gift of listening, of simply paying careful attention to what he says. In fact, listening is perhaps *the* key to gaining greater and greater intimacy with the one you love. Like a flower opening to the warmth of the sun, your partner will open his heart when you demonstrate understanding through active listening.

To realize the benefit of Proverbs 18:13, let me suggest you develop this habit: Before responding to your spouse's words with your own ideas, make sure you demonstrate that you have really heard him. Begin your feedback with a phrase such as "Are you saying…" or "What I'm hearing you say is…," then paraphrase his main idea and any emotions you perceive. Pause to listen *before* you answer.

If I had taken time to listen to Naomi that day, I would have avoided a bit of folly. Perhaps you've experienced a similar event in your own marriage. Why not make the decision now to listen to your spouse before speaking? It will make all the difference in the world.

REFLECTIONS: Share with each other the times you have felt most affirmed in conversations with each other. Did you feel affirmed because you knew your spouse was listening to you?

PRAYER FOCUS: Pray for a listening ear, for greater intimacy with each other, and for the ability to clearly *demonstrate* that you're listening to the one you love.

4

RARE AND BEAUTIFUL TREASURES

By wisdom a house is built, and through understanding it is
established; through knowledge its rooms are filled
with rare and beautiful treasures.

PROVERBS 24:3–4

Living isn't getting any cheaper, is it? Job responsibilities escalate, and chores multiply, but there never seems to be more money! When you look around, everyone but you seems to be getting ahead. You can easily grow a bit discouraged, thinking *What have I got to show for all my hard work?*

Most of us would agree that there are more important things in life than a late-model car or a new washing machine, but when we look at our bank balances we find it difficult to remember what. When I suffer from this type of amnesia, I think of my friends Jim and Laurel, parents of eight children. Jim is a schoolteacher; Laurel is a mom and a home schooler and runs a small business from their home. While God has blessed them financially in many ways, this hard-working couple don't possess a bulging bank account or massive mutual fund holdings.

So why do they provide a good reality check for me? Because they have a home filled with rare and beautiful treasures. They and their children experience a happy home, and if you could see them you'd see instantly the richness of their family.

What are the rare and beautiful treasures that this and other wise families develop in their homes?

The treasure of unconditional love. When a family fashions a place of unconditional love for everyone, it becomes a refuge from life's storms. In the world rejection is the norm, but in the family people care deeply for one another. When children experience

21

home as a place where they're loved and cherished *apart* from their performance, that unconditional love gives them the security they need to grow and thrive. It provides the sense of worth they need to move confidently into the world.

The treasure of acceptance. When it's a safe place, the family provides the perfect environment for learning attitudes, skills, and values. A healthy family tolerates mistakes, expects growth, and fosters acceptance. In the family, children develop manners and learn to respect people and property. Parents set limits and enforce them, but they also extend acceptance to each child. It's the perfect environment for the laboratory of life because when people in a family make mistakes, no one gives up on them.

The treasure of faith. I have observed, in our home and in countless others, that when parents model faith and love for God, children tend to follow that example. Day in and day out, children see spiritual realities lived out. They learn to love God and live by His values. Such a family can face each day with confidence and can weather any storm.

What's more valuable than a balanced portfolio? Homes in which wisdom, understanding, and knowledge produce these and other rare and beautiful treasures. Stop and take inventory of your most important assets, the treasures that make your home a wonderful place to live and grow. Such assets won't pay your next grocery bill, but they will certainly bring joy and happiness to your home.

REFLECTIONS: Do the treasures of unconditional love, acceptance, and faith thrive in your home? What other treasures make your home a special place? Go ahead—brag a little!

PRAYER FOCUS: Give God thanks for the many good gifts He brings to your home, then ask for insight as you parent your children. Ask God to enable you to work together to develop these treasures in your home.

5
SEEK FIRST
TO UNDERSTAND

The purposes of a man's heart are deep waters,
but a man of understanding draws them out.
PROVERBS 20:5

Maybe you've experienced or observed this phenomenon in business contacts, in church groups, and even in your marriage: Instead of directing your energy toward the person across from you—really trying to understand her—you push for her to understand you. You speak longer, louder, more vehemently about your own concerns, asking her to see from your point of view. The result? You may actually push the other person away. Instead of fostering a closer relationship, you risk growing more distant.

Proverbs 20:5 gives a solution to this problem and introduces a solid principle for relationships of all kinds: Seek first to understand, then to be understood. This sounds a little cockeyed, doesn't it? And it goes against the grain. But it's true. One of the best ways to foster a good relationship is to work hard at drawing the other person out, helping her to feel understood.

If you understand and practice this principle, you'll reap a tangible reward. When you seek first to understand your spouse, you create a safe environment, and she'll reward you with her deepest thoughts. As you accept her ideas, you encourage her to go to the next level of self-disclosure, and she'll progressively reveal more and more of herself to you. You'd be surprised at what your partner will say to you if she knows that you'll try to understand and accept what she says.

When you show your partner that you care about her thoughts and feelings, you give her a unique gift. And when your partner feels listened to and understood, she'll automatically want to listen to you, too.

Hard to believe? Then try an experiment. The next time you have a conversation with your spouse, listen carefully. Ask questions that will help you understand her position; for example, "How did you feel when that happened?" or "What's the hardest thing about this problem for you?" Give direct eye contact. Be attentive. Forget about providing solutions. Do everything you can to understand without concerning yourself about communicating your own views. Then watch what happens.

I'll tell you two things that will probably take place. First, your spouse will keep talking. She'll say more and at deeper levels when you demonstrate your desire to understand. In addition, your partner will eventually want to hear your views. She will ask you what you think. When you seek first to understand, you almost always find that you are better understood.

Check it out. Let the truth of this proverb finds its way into your marriage. Draw out the deep waters of your partner and grow closer as a result.

REFLECTIONS: Do you usually feel understood by your partner? If so, affirm her right now by describing a recent time in which it happened. If not, talk gently about how your spouse can listen to you more effectively.

PRAYER FOCUS: Ask God to give each of you a listening ear and the motivation to seek first to understand.

6
RUNNING THE RACE

Therefore, since we are surrounded by such a great cloud of witnesses,
let us throw off everything that hinders and the sin that so easily
entangles, and let us run with perseverance the race marked
out for us. Let us fix our eyes on Jesus.

HEBREWS 12:1–2

Need a bit of encouragement? Found the going tough recently? I understand. Running the race of life isn't easy.

I exercise most mornings during the week. The first part of my routine seems easy because I'm not yet tired. And I can bear the last part because I see the end in sight. It's the middle I mind. The middle of any athletic contest is often the hardest because it requires perseverance.

I think Paul must have understood this when he wrote to the Hebrew Christians, "Let us run with perseverance the race marked out for us." He was writing to Christians in the middle of the race, their spiritual journey.

We run the race too. But we don't run a sprint. No, it's more like a marathon. I have more than one friend who has run a twenty-six-mile marathon. Like life, it takes training, strategy, and extraordinary endurance. When running a marathon, you always face the danger of coming to the end of your physical resources and simply not being able to go on. My friends tell me this is called "hitting the wall." That's the danger Paul talks about: hitting a spiritual wall and coming to the end of our endurance, letting the difficulties and the challenges of life defeat us.

Fortunately, Paul provides some help for this spiritual journey. First, he reminds us that others have run the race successfully before we even stepped onto the course. I often feel encouraged when I read or hear of believers who have overcome challenges and persevered in their faith. Daniel and Joseph are two of my favorite Bible characters for that reason. Those two men knew how to run with perseverance. And since they proved it could be done, I feel encouraged to do it too.

Paul also reminds us of our need to reject anything that hinders us spiritually, especially sin. He exhorts us to avoid allowing sin to entangle us as we run the race. I once saw a runner actually trip on his own shoelaces. In the same way but at a far worse level, sin will trip us up in the race of life.

Finally, Paul shares the most important strategy of all: During the race of life, we must keep our eyes squarely on Jesus Christ. If we keep our eyes on the One who can help us, we're far less likely to stray off course or quit.

When my son was six years old, he fell down as he was running and scraped himself pretty badly. We thought it best not to bandage the sore. Jon was very brave, but throughout the afternoon he kept looking at that scrape. By evening he was a bit teary, and the scrape seemed to hurt more. Just before bedtime, Jon made a profound observation: "You know, Dad, the more you look at your owies, the more they hurt."

When we keep our eyes focused on life's pain, challenges, and difficulties, we can easily become drained of hope. But when we keep our eyes on Jesus, He renews our strength and restores our hope.

Are you in the middle of life's race and facing a challenge? Don't give up. Instead, take some encouragement from a fellow runner: With God's help, we can run with perseverance.

REFLECTIONS: When was the last time you felt as if you'd hit the wall spiritually? How can you encourage each other to run the race with perseverance when you feel like quitting?

PRAYER FOCUS: Pray together for God to give you endurance as you run the race He has called you to.

7
BUILDING A MARRIAGE

The wise woman builds her house.

PROVERBS 14:1

Have you ever felt inadequate as a marriage partner? Most of us do from time to time. The daily demands of building a healthy marriage can sometimes feel overwhelming. You've been there, haven't you? You've probably experienced times when you think, *Am I ever going to get it?*

Consider this bit of encouragement: Building a marriage is not an event; it's a process. A wise wife spends a lifetime building her marriage; a wise husband does the same.

For me, the most important observation about this building process is that it is *willful.* You build a marriage by making a series of choices each day about your words, actions, and attitudes. Regardless of what happens in your life, you can always choose to speak a kind word or listen attentively. These choices reflect committed love and build the marriage bond.

The building process is also *intentional.* The first thing a builder does as he prepares to build a house is study the blueprints. The building process can't go well unless the builder knows where he is going. Marriage builders also need to know where they're going in the process and be aware of the "tools and materials" necessary for the job.

As far as I know, you can't purchase a complete set of marital blueprints anywhere. You can, however, find many Scripture passages and scripturally based books that offer instruction. In addition, most of us know some "master builders," veteran couples with sound marriages whose examples and encouragement provide important tips about the building process. I encourage you to tap into these resources whenever you can.

The building process is not only willful and intentional; it is also *continual*. You may think, *Hey, we've been married a long time. The foundation, superstructure, and even the finishing touches of our marital house are well in place. Everything's just fine.* Not so fast! Even if you think you've completed the building phase, you still have maintenance work to do. My physical house was finished years ago, but it takes unbelievable effort to maintain it. My shake roof looks good, but if I don't inspect the shingles and check for rot every year, I'm asking for trouble. I clean the aggregate sidewalk once a year, but before I know it, moss begins to grow again.

Life's downward pull is constant. Owning a house means working hard against that pull. Homeowners have to pay that price if they want to enjoy a beautiful home year in and year out. In the same way, healthy marriages need maintenance too. No matter how long you've been married, you always face that downward pull. Your relationship needs constant attention. There's always something in our marriages to shore up, clean up, or build up: a new lesson to learn, a skill to perfect, or an attitude to foster.

The next time you feel inadequate, remember that marriage is not an event; it's a process. If today wasn't so good, plan to make tomorrow better. Get used to asking yourself, *What's one small step I can take today that will build my marriage?* Then go for it!

REFLECTIONS: What have you done recently to build up your relationship? Have you read a book on marriage? shared a weekend away? established a new hobby together? prayed as a couple? What steps could you take to build or maintain your relationship in the months ahead?

PRAYER FOCUS: Invite God to help you understand how to build your marriage relationship.

8
THE FRONT LINES
OF LOVE

Love never fails.

1 CORINTHIANS 13:8

Like most of us, you've probably experienced this scenario: A well-known and loved couple announce that they're getting divorced, and you sit staring in disbelief. *No! Not these two.* The words of that country western song float through your mind: "Doesn't anybody stay together anymore?"

Failed love. There are many reasons for it, and only God can judge each situation. But Christian couples needn't fall into the trap of thinking that a good marriage happens by chance or that the factors leading to divorce invade a home like a virus, seeping into a relationship with no warning or remedy. We needn't fear that one day we will fall into the whirlpool of a failed marriage.

In fact, our Father tells us, "Love never fails." Or as J. B. Phillips puts it, "Love knows no limit to its endurance." Your love for your spouse need never fail.

Too simple, you say? Simple? Yes. Easy? No. Here are some of my favorite words on the subject:

> To be married is not to be taken off the front lines of love, but rather to be plunged into the thick of things. It is to be faced, day in and day out, with the necessity of making over and over again, and at deeper and deeper levels, that same terrifyingly momentous and impossible decision which one could only have made when one was head-over-heels in love and out of one's mind with trust and faith.... Is it any wonder if people cannot take the pressure? It is a pressure that can only be handled by love, and

29

in ever increasing doses. Marriage involves a continuous daily renewal of a decision which, since it is of such a staggering order as to be humanly impossible to make, can only be made through the grace of God.[1]

Is there a preventive for failed marital love? Yes: a "continuous daily renewal," a series of decisions to do what love dictates. It's tempting to retreat to the comfort of self, but you must not give yourself that luxury. Stay on the front lines of love—that's where the action is. It's where hard decisions are made and victories are won.

You may ask, What about relationship pain? What about our inability to stay focused over the long haul? That's where God's grace comes in. None of us can make these choices without God's enabling power at work in us. The task is impossible without Him.

As you start this day, make the choice to stay on the front lines of love. Then think how you can practically demonstrate such love to your partner. Finally, commit yourself into God's hands for His divine enabling as you make choice after choice to stay on the front lines of love. With God's help, love won't fail.

PRAYER FOCUS: No discussion today; just prayer. Renew your decision before God to stay on the front lines of love. Ask God to give you grace to do the very best for your spouse every day. At the end of your prayer time, if you can, turn to your spouse and verbalize your commitment to love him.

9
THE GRACE FACTOR

For we do not have a high priest who is unable to sympathize with
our weaknesses, but we have one who has been tempted in
every way, just as we are—yet was without sin.
Let us then approach the throne of grace with confidence, so that we
may receive mercy and find grace to help us in our time of need.

HEBREWS 4:15–16

There I was again, on my knees asking God to forgive me, knowing I had failed exactly this way more times than I could count. Because I felt distant from God, I also felt distant from my wife. When the relationship with God is hindered, all other important relationships suffer too.

Perhaps you've been there. You've lost your temper or entertained a wrong thought or yielded again to some weakness, and afterward you've felt separated from God. *How could God forgive me?* you think. For an hour or a day or a week, you look up, seeking God, and feel as if the heavens are slate gray, silent and uninviting.

We all know we aren't what we *want* to be. And something in us finds it hard to believe that we are redeemable. We see our sin sickness and wonder how God can overlook a black heart. Does He accept us in the depths of our imperfection?

Oh, we've *heard* that He does, but at times we aren't convinced. We believe it's true, but sometimes we don't feel it. We expect any moment to receive an eviction notice from heaven. Self-doubt bores into our hearts like a poisonous thorn, spreading its venom into our spiritual blood stream.

At such times, we long for assurance that God accepts us.

We have that assurance in these sixty or so words from

Hebrews. Two thoughts cut through everything else in this passage: (1) Jesus understands our temptations and weaknesses, and (2) He invites us to come boldly before God despite our failures to find forgiveness for our sins and help with our problems.

We're talking about the grace factor, God's unlimited love and total acceptance. Our Lord understands us, even our darkest secrets, and accepts us still.

Do we slink up to God's throne, expecting condemnation? No way! Miraculously, we come with full confidence into God's presence. Like little children, we run and jump into our Father's lap, knowing He will hold us close and whisper words of assurance and love.

It all seems too good to be true, doesn't it? Compassion and love, mercy and grace—this is God's promise to His children. God's invitation stands; come with full assurance. Glorious words for His imperfect children.

What about you? Feeling unforgiven? In need of God's acceptance? Tempted to give up? Find the assurance you need in these words: "Let us then approach the throne of grace with confidence."

REFLECTIONS: Do you sometimes feel separated from God? How can you help each other appropriate God's grace at such times?
PRAYER FOCUS: Ask your Father for reassurance of His grace when you fail, for help in receiving His gift of forgiveness, and for strength to stay connected both to God and to each other during these times.

10
LIGHTEN UP!

A cheerful heart is good medicine.

PROVERBS 17:22

Naomi and I were lying in bed the other night, chuckling over something that had happened that day. The lights were off and the kids in bed, so we didn't want to make too much noise. We cuddled closer and whispered. Naomi said something that tickled me, and laughing, I responded with some quip. The giggling started, and squeaks of suppressed laughter escaped our lips. Finally, we gave up and surrendered to wave after wave of laughter. When we could laugh no more, we lay still in each other's arms, smiling into the darkness, feeling warm, contented, and renewed.

King Solomon said it without embellishment: "A cheerful heart is good medicine." Applied to couples, I'd phrase it this way: "Shared laughter is a positive prescription for any marriage."

Anyone married longer than three minutes knows that married life inevitably brings challenges. Crises, transitions, and difficulties surface, demanding our attention. Of course, communication and conflict-resolution skills certainly help couples navigate life's problems. But couples too often overlook one more element necessary for successfully managing the storms of life: a sense of humor.

Choosing to see the lighter side makes marriage a lot easier. A sense of humor eases tension, gives perspective, joins couples in the intimacy of a shared experience, and often clears the mind and heart, helping couples solve their problems.

Many times my wife and I have laughed at ourselves. When my oldest girl was a preschooler, I was playing with her one evening while Naomi sat close by. When it was time to get ready for bed, I said, "Okay, time for bed. You need to put on your jammies."

"No," our daughter said, smiling but putting her hands on her hips.

"Who's in charge around here, anyway?" I said, keeping it light.

Without hesitation she replied, "Mommy."

Naomi and I looked at each other and convulsed with laughter. Daddy apparently wasn't projecting a powerful, "in charge" persona to his little girl!

When people have been less than kind, when circumstances have looked grim, when we've made mistakes, when life has been inconvenient, we've laughed. Our laughter has never solved a problem, but it has made our journey toward solutions a great deal easier.

Couples, lighten up! Go ahead, laugh at yourselves. See the humor in each situation. Allow yourselves a smile. Choose today to see the lighter side. As you do, King Solomon's "medicine" will flow, helping bring health and wholeness to your marriage.

REFLECTIONS: Do you presently face a difficult challenge? Do you need to lighten up in the midst of it? How can you encourage each other to move in this direction?

PRAYER FOCUS: Pray for the gift of laughter, for the ability to see humor on the road of life, especially in difficult times.

11
PARENTS IN PROCESS

*Folly is bound up in the heart of a child, but the rod
of discipline will drive it far from him.*

PROVERBS 22:15

Parenting is a tough job, isn't it? In fact, the potential for disaster
feels titanic. If you have children, without a doubt you've made
mistakes. That's why it's best to view parenting as a process, a set of
skills and attitudes that you develop over time. A parent in
process—that's me.

When my first child was young, I had to fight against a recurring problem: You see, I was a softy. I found it hard to give my
daughter the discipline she needed, especially when it came to corporal punishment. When my four-year-old girl looked up at me,
catching her breath between sobs, I melted. I wasn't nearly as consistent as Naomi, who seemed the quintessential parent.

My lack of consistency drove me to prayer. I remember one
especially important conversation with the Lord. "God," I said, "I
just love my little girl. I don't want to hurt her."

Surprisingly, the Lord dropped a thought into my heart:
"You're thinking about *your* pain, not hers."

As soon as this thought came, I instantly identified it as the
truth. I was thinking about how difficult the discipline process was
for *me*, the pain *I* endured when I had to spank or enforce other
consequences with my little girl.

But God wasn't finished with me yet. As I pondered what God
seemed to say, a second truth bomb went off inside my mind: If I
failed to discipline my child, she would fail to grow up socially,
emotionally, and spiritually, and it would be *my* responsibility.

That's when I remembered Proverbs 22:15: "Folly is bound up

in the heart of a child...." I needed to remember that my little Jenny was foolish. All kids come into the world that way. Foolishness has to do with a child's mistaken notion that she must have her own way, and further, that things will be *better* if she has her own way. Talk about foolish! If I allowed Jenny to grow up without driving foolishness out, she would never learn to accept authority, to think of others, or to control herself.

Judge Robert Bork once said it this way: "Every new generation constitutes a wave of savages who must be civilized by their families, schools, and churches."[1] As a father himself, Bork was certainly having a bit of fun, but "civilizing the savages" isn't a bad way to view parenting!

So how do we parents civilize our kids? We drive out foolishness by setting healthy limits and enforcing them. Discipline must happen within an all-pervading atmosphere of love, but it must happen. Setting limits and enforcing them as consistently as possible—that's the parental task. We can't allow our children to win the battle of wills. If they win, they, in reality, lose.

That's what God impressed on me so many years ago. I've learned a lot more over the years but nothing as basic to the parenting task.

Perhaps, like me, you're at a teachable moment as a parent. Good! We parents-in-process will always have a lesson we need to learn, and we can always count on God to help us grow.

REFLECTIONS: Share with each other the area of parenting that you find the most difficult. Do you feel that you're in process in that area? If not, what will help you start to grow?
PRAYER FOCUS: Ask each other for specific ways you can pray for one another as parents. Then do it!

12
RECOVERING FROM
MISTAKES

*And we know that in all things God works for the good of those who
love him, who have been called according to his purpose.*

ROMANS 8:28

Have you ever messed up badly—I mean *badly?* Ever made an
unintentional mistake at work, home, or school so inept, so clumsy,
so devoid of merit that you wondered how you'd ever recover from
it?

I remember making this type of mistake more than twenty
years ago. As a first-year high school teacher, I had limited teacher
training and virtually no experience. I was a fresh-faced, twenty-
two-year-old bundle of naiveté.

Perhaps I had heard the advice: "Don't smile 'til Christmas," but
I had certainly failed to heed it. As a result, I was in deep trouble with
my ninth-grade English class in the area professionals call "classroom control."

I decided one day to help the kids realize how disruptive they
were. It was just the kind of strategy my methods professor had
told me would work with high schoolers of the '70s. In fact, I took
the idea from one of my old textbooks.

I decided to do a role play. I'd play a student for a few minutes,
and one of them would play the teacher. In so doing, my students
would learn how difficult it is to run a class. I exchanged places
with one of my pubescent charges and sat down at his desk. When
the student took his place in front, I did what I had seen various
students do for weeks. I rolled up a piece of paper and threw it at
the wastepaper basket just in front of where the "teacher" stood.

The other students stared with unbelieving eyes for half a second. Then, as if guided by one voice, they crumpled up paper and

various other items and threw them at each other with the wild abandon of escaped zoo animals. Within three seconds, the room was a madhouse of spit wads, paper airplanes, and unidentifiable flying objects.

Just as I realized I had made a mistake of gigantic proportions, I glanced through the window of my classroom door and saw one of the school counselors staring at us in shocked amazement.

Did I recover from this mistake? You bet. I had a great second year and did indeed learn how to control a classroom. God used this experience to help me develop as a teacher. He used it to keep me humble and to remind me that I was totally dependent on Him. He brought my wife and me closer as we discussed and prayed about this and other first-year problems. Finally, He gave me a lifelong appreciation for public schoolteachers!

You see, God takes even our mistakes—notice the "all things" in Romans 8:28—and weaves them into life's tapestry for our good. If we'll admit our faults and ask God for wisdom, He'll use our mistakes as a teaching aid to help us develop into the people He wants us to be. If you're still cringing from a recent mistake, take heart. In *all* things, God works for good!

REFLECTIONS: Do you remember a mistake that has caused you pain? Can you see the good God has brought from it?

PRAYER FOCUS: Invite God to give you grateful hearts even in the midst of difficulty. Ask Him for grace to recover from mistakes, for tolerance with each other in the race of life, and for the ability to encourage each other when you stumble.

13
POSITIVE THINKING AND YOUR MARRIAGE

Whatever is true, whatever is noble, whatever is right,
whatever is pure, whatever is lovely, whatever is admirable—if
anything is excellent or praiseworthy—think about such things.
PHILIPPIANS 4:8

Have you monitored your thought life recently? If not, you may be missing a great opportunity to improve your marriage. A positive thought life is the linchpin of a satisfying relationship.

What you think has a tremendous impact on what you feel and how you act. This is particularly true in the daily give and take between a husband and a wife. When your partner acts, you react. Your thoughts, however, determine what your reaction will be.

Let me give you an example. While my wife was walking with friends recently, I decided to wash the dishes and clean the kitchen. It was my day off and I wanted to make her day easier. When Naomi returned, she began home schooling the kids and didn't acknowledge what I had done. In fact, she didn't notice it all day! At first I thought negatively: *I spent all that time, and she didn't even notice!* But after a while, I caught myself. *Hold it...she's busy. She is grateful for the ways I help her. Her mind is just on other things.*

Had I stayed with the first line of inner dialogue, I would have felt hurt and angry and might have withdrawn. My negative thoughts would have led to negative feelings and then to negative actions. Instead, because I shifted my mind to what was true and right, my emotions and actions were positive.

Do you see why Philippians 4:8 is so important to your marriage? What you allow to occupy your mind will influence your feelings, words, and actions. What you think about your partner

39

and your relationship will nudge its way into your marriage whether you like it or not.

Of course, you don't have to ignore your partner's negative behavior. After all, Philippians 4:8 advocates keeping our minds and hearts centered on what is true. God doesn't tell us to ignore what's really there. But our Father *does* tell us not to occupy our minds with negatives, to stew in our anger, or to allow our partner's weaknesses to become our primary focus.

Sometime during this day and the days to come, monitor your thinking about your spouse or something your spouse has done. Then evaluate those thoughts in light of this list: whatever is true, noble, right, pure, lovely, admirable, excellent, or praiseworthy. Pause a moment and ask God to help you choose His thoughts and His perspective. Make this a habit, then watch as your marriage relationship grows.

REFLECTIONS: As a way of encouraging God's perspective, affirm each other right now. Tell your partner what you see in him that's true, noble, right, pure, lovely, admirable, excellent, or praiseworthy. For the rest of the day, focus on at least one of those qualities, thanking God for what you see in your spouse.

PRAYER FOCUS: Pray for the ability to dwell on the positive in each other and in your relationship. Ask God to help you change your emotions and actions by first changing your thoughts.

14
BECAUSE YOU SAY SO, LORD

When he had finished speaking, he said to Simon,
"Put out into deep water, and let down the nets for a catch."
Simon answered, "Master, we've worked hard all night and haven't
caught anything. But because you say so, I will let down the nets."
LUKE 5:4–5

How-to books abound these days. Everybody seems to have just the solution for enjoying a successful life and a fulfilled marriage. Maybe you're confused at times about which direction to go or even about what success might mean to God.

Luke 5 simplifies the equation considerably. Simon Peter and his companions had been fishing all night. They were cleaning their nets with the tired resignation of workers near the end of a long workday. They were tired, dirty, and probably irritable since they hadn't caught anything. Jesus walked into the middle of this scene with a simple request: "Push out farther and put down your nets."

This must have made absolutely no sense to Simon Peter. He tried to explain, "We've worked hard all night and haven't caught anything." What was Jesus thinking? "You know that the best time to fish is at night. The sun has just pushed the fish deeper into the lake. Right now is the *worst* time of day to fish." I'm sure Simon Peter was tempted to argue or simply to say, "I'm tired."

But instead of arguing, Simon Peter said something so significant that it has captured the attention of Christians for generations: "But because you say so, I will let down the nets." You know the rest of the story. The result of Simon Peter's obedience extended far beyond his wildest dreams.

Do you want to simplify the formula for success in life?

Become a "because You say so" Christian. Do you want to enjoy success in your marriage? Become a "because You say so" Christian.

"Lord, it sure is difficult to love my spouse sometimes, but because You say so, I will."

"I'm not sure how to forgive this hurt, but because You say so, I'll do it."

"It sure is difficult to go to church every week, but because You say so, I'll go."

"I'm not sure how teaching Sunday school to sixth-grade boys will work, but because You say so, I'll volunteer."

"Because You say so" Christians follow one rule: simple obedience to God. Our barriers to success have little to do with a lack of truth; they more often involve an unwillingness to *obey* the truth God has already provided, particularly in the Bible. We can find 90 percent of God's will for our lives in His Word. The Bible details how to treat our spouses; it provides solutions to relationship problems; it even outlines how to manage our businesses or personal finances.

What does it take to enjoy the benefits of obeying God's truth? A series of choices. Over and over we say to God, "because *You* say so." That's about the simplest how-to you'll ever find for success in all areas of your life, including your marriage.

REFLECTIONS: Have you found it difficult to obey God in some areas over the last several weeks? How has this affected your daily life? your marriage? What's one area about which you need to say "because You say so" to God? What follow-up action will that require in the coming days?

PRAYER FOCUS: Ask God to forgive you for the times you've stubbornly resisted His will. Ask for a renewed motivation to be a "because You say so" Christian and enjoy the benefits of obedience.

15
FORGIVENESS 101

Above all, love each other deeply, because love covers
over a multitude of sins.

1 PETER 4:8

Listen to these words about marriage from Mike Mason's book *The Mystery of Marriage:* "What is hard about marriage…is the strain of living continually in the light of a conscience other than our own, being under the intimate scrutiny of another pair of eyes."[1]

Mason is absolutely right. Married life reveals both your strengths and weaknesses to the one you love. Experiencing the former is a joy; the latter can be decidedly painful. Blind spots, annoying habits, weaknesses, and sins will surface in even the most mature person. And you cannot hide these things from the searchlight of your partner's gaze.

My wife could give you quite a list of my faults. For example, she knows that I'm not detail-oriented. I can't tell you how many times I've forgotten some task she has asked me to do, such as picking up something from the grocery store or making a phone call. Irritating. I also have a constitutional belief that everything will work out in life, so sometimes I decline to plan as thoroughly as my wife might prefer. Exasperating. To top it off, my sense of humor can sometimes erupt into silliness. Embarrassing. I could go on.

How does Naomi put up with me? Good question.

There *is* a clear danger that exists in living with an imperfect partner. Offenses may accumulate. Whether these flaws are slightly irritating or major headaches, they can accrue over time. If you're not careful, unforgiveness may burrow its way under your emotional skin and spill its poison into your marriage.

So how *do* two imperfect people live together? How do they bear each other's "intimate scrutiny"?

There's only one solution: They must learn to "cover in love." Partners must love each other so deeply that their love covers each other's sins. You know what I mean. Your husband wakes up feeling irritable and is short with you. Your wife forgets to mail the house payment. Your husband is delayed and forgets to call. Life is full of such aggravations. For some, these are only the tip of the iceberg.

Obviously, you may need to communicate about such difficulties, but it's even more important to learn to overlook your partner's faults and to let them go. If Naomi makes a mistake or displays a weakness, I have a choice to make. I can either hold onto that hard knot of unforgiveness and sustain my anger, or I can forgive. The first means pain and bitterness and stress; the second, love and joy and peace.

In healthy marriages, love makes a series of choices to overlook trespasses. As Christ has forgiven us, we are to forgive our spouses. Such love does more to break potential tension between partners than almost anything else.

What about you? Do you find yourself holding onto the little things? Let them go. Cover in love, and forgive. It's one of the best things you can do for the one you love.

REFLECTIONS: Do you feel "covered" in your marriage? Does it feel safe to make a mistake? Or do you allow little things to inordinately affect your relationship? Is there an issue right now that you need to release?

PRAYER FOCUS: Invite God to give you forgiving hearts and fervent, unconditional love for each other.

16
FORGIVENESS 201

*Then Peter came to Jesus and asked, "Lord, how many times shall I
forgive my brother when he sins against me? Up to seven times?"
Jesus answered, "I tell you, not seven times,
but seventy-seven times."*

MATTHEW 18:21–22

Love covers a multitude of sins. But what about those issues
between a husband and wife that go beyond an aggravating attitude or an irritating habit? What if harsh words are more common
than they should be? What if personality differences frequently
cause friction? What if you've been hurt more than once and feel
you have a raw emotional nerve exposed much of the time? How
does one "cover in love" in these more difficult circumstances?

Peter asked Jesus a similar question. He was obviously thinking about a person in his life who was close enough to do some
damage. Thinking he was being magnanimous, Peter suggested
that forgiving someone seven times ought to be plenty. Imagine his
surprise when essentially Jesus said, "No, you need to forgive someone as many times as it takes."

Jesus must have seen the incredulous look on Peter's face
because He proceeded to tell a story to help the disciple understand
His statement. As a communicator, Jesus has no equal, and the
parable of the unmerciful servant is a masterpiece, packing an
enormous spiritual wallop. It has helped generations of believers
grasp one of the most vital principles in all of God's Word: the
importance of forgiveness.

It's a simple story, really. The servant with a debt of millions
had virtually no hope of paying up, but the compassionate king forgave the entire debt. But when this same servant had the

opportunity to forgive his fellow servant a ten-dollar debt, he decided to send his fellow servant to jail.

As the details of the story unfold, we find ourselves feeling angry at the injustice of it all. We want the king to find out and punish the unmerciful servant, and the faster the better. When the confrontation happens, we feel so gratified. The king tells the servant, "I canceled all that debt of yours…shouldn't you have had mercy on your fellow servant…?" Then (and oh, is it sweet) the king has the servant thrown into jail where he belongs. Good riddance!

Only then do we find that we've been set up. God is the king, and all of us, His servants. Since each of us has been freely forgiven a debt we can never repay, we must forgive our fellow servants their infinitely smaller debts. To decide not to forgive is to be tortured in a prison of bitterness.

The parable reduces each of us to silence. Our rage at the unmerciful servant is turned inward as we consider our own hardness of heart.

How this parable applies to marriage! Has your husband been insensitive recently? Has your wife failed to support you in a new venture? Have hard words been spoken between you? You have a choice to make. Will you forgive? Will you release your spouse from the debt as God has released you?

"What about our responsibility to communicate and resolve conflict?" you ask. We need to do that, too, but first we must release the debt. "As many as seven times?" No. As many times as it takes.

REFLECTIONS: If you can, share with each other right now instances in which you have had difficulty forgiving others. Has that spilled over into your marriage relationship?
PRAYER FOCUS: Ask God to give you a soft heart and to help you choose to forgive each other whenever difficult situations arise.

17
PRACTICAL FORGIVENESS

*Be kind and compassionate to one another, forgiving each other,
just as in Christ God forgave you.*

EPHESIANS 4:32

In every marriage—and I do mean *every* marriage—husbands and
wives do and say things that offend their partners. Usually, such an
offense is something small, such as a missed appointment or a
thoughtless remark. Since the pain is slight, forgiveness is easy to
extend in these situations.

Occasionally, however, something more serious happens. A
spouse deeply offends her partner and causes tremendous pain.
That offense cuts deeply into her husband's heart and mind. At
those times, forgiving is not so easy.

In situations like these, have you ever thought, *I want to forgive,
but I don't know how. I've said the words, but I still have the same feelings.* Many of us have felt this way at one time or another. So what
do you do when forgiveness doesn't come naturally? What does it
mean, practically, to forgive? Maybe taking the following steps will
help.

1. Assess the debt. If your spouse has offended you, she is, in a
sense, in "debt" to you. If you brush off the hurt without processing
it, the pain will surface again and again when you least expect it.
That's why you need to assess the debt. If you find yourself need-
ing to forgive your spouse, sit down and describe in writing the way
or ways in which your spouse has offended you. Really give it some
thought. By assessing the debt and understanding it, you'll have a
clear sense of what you need to give to the Lord.

2. Forgive the debt. Perhaps the hardest part of the forgiveness
process is choosing to let go of the debt. However, since Christ has

forgiven you, you must do the same for your partner. When you're ready, take your list of "debts," hold it up to God, and say, "Lord, you have forgiven me a great debt. Now I choose to forgive my spouse a debt as well." Then tear up the list. Choose to forgive and be free.

3. *Don't replay the hurt.* Choosing to forgive is only the beginning. In the forgiveness process, you have to make another important decision. You must choose to avoid replaying the hurt in your mind. You know what I'm talking about: that mental recording of the hurtful event. Over and over, you see the situation in your mind and feel the pain again. Instead, when tempted to relive the experience, interrupt your thoughts. Declare again, "I have forgiven my spouse, and I will not replay what I've already forgiven." Then go to God, asking for His help in moving on.

Many people don't take this step. If you don't, you can find yourself back in a morass of pain and bitterness. Your anger will be sustained month after month, year after year.

4. *Continue to forgive.* You may have to carry out steps one through three many times in your marriage. After all, you live with a human being. People usually change slowly, and you'll have ample opportunity to learn how to apply God's Word: "Be kind and compassionate to one another, forgiving each other, just as in Christ God forgave you."

Is there anything you need to forgive each other for right now? If so, I encourage you to take these four steps. Forgive each other just as God has forgiven you.

REFLECTIONS: Talking about this can be difficult but has real value. If you've ever withheld forgiveness, confess that to your spouse. Make sure that you have a clean slate with each other.
PRAYER FOCUS: Ask God to help you forgive when you need to. Ask Him to help you make choices that reflect kindness and compassion.

18
THE PARTNERSHIP
OF CHANGE

And we…are being transformed into his likeness with ever-increasing
glory, which comes from the Lord, who is the Spirit.
2 CORINTHIANS 3:18

Just when I think I've reached a point of consistency in my spiritual walk, I find myself saying or doing something which proves I have abundant room left for growth. At such times I think, *Will I ever get this right?*

One such problem surfaces and resurfaces every now and then like an enemy submarine, its menacing presence a reminder of my imperfection. What is it? Impatience. Oh, I'm not impatient about everything. In fact, in some situations I'm quite good at waiting. But some things just get to me—things like waiting for appointments with doctors, waiting in line, and traffic that seems never to move. Whenever I think my time is being wasted, I can feel tension and irritation rising to the surface.

When this and other areas of weakness arise, I'm tempted to give up. Sometimes I feel overwhelmed by a particular spiritual deficit and incapable of making a change. After all, change is hard. Our flesh is notoriously resistant to it.

Regardless of my feelings at the time, however, I know I'm wrong about my seeming inability to change. Change is a part of God's plan for my life. According to 2 Corinthians 3:18, gradual change—becoming more like Jesus every day—is God's plan for *every* believer's life. Transformation is our destiny. In a sense, we've all enrolled in a lifelong apprenticeship, learning to be like Christ from one day to the next. The Spirit Himself helps in this process, placing His hand on ours, guiding us as we learn to imitate our Lord.

So how do we change? While the Spirit works in us for positive change, believers have a definite part to play in the process. For example, when I've decided to pray in the midst of my impatience, asking Him to help me exhibit self-control, I've felt His strength surge within me, enabling me to keep perspective. In addition to prayer, I've also chosen to monitor my thinking and make sure I act on God's truth.

Change involves working with God. It's a partnership. We act; God empowers. We cooperate with the Spirit; He supplies what we need. Positive change is not a solo performance. Alone we may lack what we need, but with God's grace and power, we will ultimately succeed.

We'll always have room to grow as Christians, but we never face the process alone. Our Father is our loving partner every step of the way.

Are you growing a little weary in the race of life? Are you tired of putting one foot in front of the other? Are you discouraged, wondering if you'll ever see growth and transformation in those troublesome areas?

Don't give up. You have a Partner who will help you. Pull close to your Father and watch what you and He can do together.

REFLECTIONS: Are you presently working on a change in your life? What are you doing to make that change happen? Have you invited God's Spirit to help you along?

PRAYER FOCUS: Invite God to help you grow in a specific area of your life. Ask God to help you cooperate with His Spirit's work for positive change.

19
PLEASANT WORDS

*Pleasant words are a honeycomb, sweet to the
soul and healing to the bones.*

PROVERBS 16:24

Perhaps you've recently received a well-placed compliment or an
affirming thank-you from your spouse. Felt good, didn't it? The
pleasant words I receive from my wife are among the most powerful and healing elements of our relationship. I think she'd probably
say the same about my positive words to her.

When you consider the negatives we encounter every day, you
understand how much each of us needs such words. The work
environment can be caustic and our society cynical. Even our own
inner voices tell us over and over again, "You're only as good as you
perform" or "You're nothing special" or "Your flaws are enormous—how could anyone love you?"

With negative voices coming from so many directions, pleasant words can remind us of God's truth in our lives. They bring joy
to our hearts and even have an effect on our physical bodies. What
amazing power we have to positively affect our spouses!

Pleasant words between couples include *words of affection.*
Compliments communicate a warmth of caring that shatters the
icy build-up of negatives around us. I recently observed a husband
telling his wife, "You have such a wonderful smile." You should
have seen her face light up with delight! When I speak affectionate
words to my wife, I can sense her spirits rise and her self-esteem
soar.

Words of acceptance boost each other's spirits, too, and are a
powerful antidote to the world's performance orientation. Such
words communicate to your spouse that you're in her corner, no

matter what. I apologized to Naomi recently for forgetting something she had asked me to pick up at the store. It's not an infrequent occurrence, because I'm not a detail-oriented person. As I walked in the door, I slapped my forehead and said to Naomi, "I'm sorry I'm so forgetful of details." Know what she said to me? "That's okay, Art. You have lots of other great qualities." Wow! Acceptance surged into my mind and heart—what an emotional lift!

Pleasant words also include *words of appreciation*. I've noticed over time that couples often stop thanking each other for performing small, everyday tasks. They stop showing appreciation for a meal cooked or a day spent at work. What a missed opportunity! An attitude of gratefulness for the variety of ways your spouse pleases you will yield an amazing harvest. Words of appreciation help your spouse feel wanted and needed. Small notes of appreciation and words of gratitude or thanks help cement the emotional bond between you and your partner. They communicate your deep feelings about your spouse. When my wife thanks me for spending time on an unpleasant household chore or for simply being a good father, I feel affirmed. I feel her approval.

Sweet to the soul and healing to the bones—that's God's promise about pleasant words. Would you like that promise to be operating in your home? Then why not spend this week taking opportunities to speak words of affection, acceptance, and appreciation to each other? You'll bring God's blessings into your home in a unique and beneficial way.

REFLECTIONS: Are pleasant words an integral part of your life together? Right now, ask each other if you have spoken words of affection, acceptance, and appreciation during the last week. If your spouse spoke such words, how did it make you feel?

PRAYER FOCUS: Ask God to help you speak pleasant words to each other regularly.

20
TO FIGHT OR
NOT TO FIGHT

It is to a man's honor to avoid strife,
but every fool is quick to quarrel.
PROVERBS 20:3

Think about the last time you experienced a conflict in your marriage. Did you find yourself getting angry? Did the conflict escalate and ignite a fire of hostile words? The Bible calls such behavior fighting or quarreling and clearly says, "Don't do that!"

Years ago, a young couple actually told me that fighting wasn't so bad because, after all, they had so much *fun* making up. Forgive me, but this kind of attitude has always struck me as rather odd. It's a little like saying, "I love to get smashed in the face because it feels so much better when the swelling goes down."

What's more, God's Word simply doesn't allow for it. Proverbs 20:3 is just one of many Scriptures that condemn quarreling. This passage cuts us no slack: "Every fool is quick to quarrel." It's a hard truth, but an important one, especially for married couples.

Notice that the Scripture says "don't *fight*," not "don't *talk*." Every couple will encounter conflict; it's simply what happens when you disagree. You may disagree about any number of subjects such as how to discipline the kids, what color to paint the living room, or where to go for vacation.

When you experience conflict, view it as an opportunity for improving your relationship. That's right; you can come out on the other side of conflict feeling closer together, not further apart. The key is how you decide to handle the conflict. Some advice? Handle each conflict by speaking directly, skillfully, and kindly.

There's a difference between communicating indirectly and directly. Indirect communication during conflict tends to be demonstrated rather than spoken. Instead of saying, "I'm feeling angry right now," you might slam a door or withdraw emotionally. When upset, avoid stuffing your feelings; go to your spouse directly and as quickly as possible. Tell him what you're experiencing. Don't let the issue fester and become worse than it is.

Learning to speak directly without blame is a key skill in preventing or resolving conflict. You can achieve this by using "I" statements instead of "you" statements. For example, *"I* feel anxious when you drive so fast," not *"You're* a reckless driver." See the difference? One places a premium on the relationship; the other does not.

Kindness also helps immeasurably when things are tense between you. It's the oil that keeps the conflict-resolution machinery lubricated as it grinds through its work. If you determine to treat your spouse with gentleness and kindness during conflict, you'll dramatically increase your ability to resolve discord. Scripture says it this way: "A gentle answer turns away wrath, but a harsh word stirs up anger" (Proverbs 15:1).

Sometime in the next few weeks, you'll probably have a conflict. I can almost guarantee it. Why not determine now how you'll handle it? Why not covenant together to speak directly, skillfully, and kindly? You'll reap the benefits of a happier, healthier relationship.

REFLECTIONS: Discuss with each other how you feel about your conflict-resolution skills. Are you doing okay in this area? If not, what do you need to improve? And how can you improve it?

PRAYER FOCUS: Ask God to help you put a priority on your relationship during times of conflict. Agree in prayer to make needed changes.

21
GOD IS IN CONTROL

*There is no wisdom, no insight, no plan
that can succeed against the LORD.*

PROVERBS 21:30

Do you wonder whether God is working His plan in your life? Let me encourage you: God is in control. In fourteen words, Proverbs 21:30 articulates one of the most important concepts found in Scripture. It's called God's sovereignty. In other words, *nothing* can overrule God's will.

I'll never forget one of the first times I saw this truth demonstrated in my adult life. It happened over twenty years ago. I was a proud, happy graduate of the University of Washington, class of '75. I was also newly married that summer and looking for my first teaching job, hoping to start that autumn.

All through college, people told me, "You're crazy to become a teacher. There's a glut of teachers on the market. You're especially crazy to think you can get a job teaching *English!*" I knew I was doing the right thing, but frankly, I didn't know if I could land a teaching job.

However, I did know what to say to people who told me, "You'll never find a teaching job." My reply? "I'll find a teaching job if God *wants* me to have a teaching job." What was I saying? That God's plan would prevail. If He had a job for me that year, I would get it.

I sent out fifty résumés that summer. I waited for calls asking for interviews. None came. The wait was not a comfortable one. Finally, one school called me for an interview. Wow, an interview! I was excited!

On the appointed day, I drove to North Kitsap High School in

Poulsbo, a small town located west of Seattle. I endured a grueling three-hour interview. By the end of the ordeal, I felt good about the interview and about my chances of landing the job. But before I walked out the door, the interviewers told me they had received two hundred applications for the job and were interviewing *twelve* other candidates after me! Suddenly the odds looked dismal for a new college graduate with no teaching experience. I had told my friends that if God wanted me to have that job, I would get it. Now my trust would be tested.

After the interview, I told the principal that I would be traveling to California during the upcoming week for a wedding. It was the week before school was supposed to start. If they wanted to reach me, I told them, they would have to call me there.

I was at my friend's apartment in Sacramento a few days later when the phone rang. "Be nice, Mike," I told him. "I could be receiving an important phone call." In a silly mood, my friend picked up the phone and said with confidence, "Mike's Bar and Grill." The caller was obviously confused, Mike told me later, but he asked for me. Mike handed me the phone; it was the principal of North Kitsap High School! He offered me the teaching position! I managed to sound professional over the phone, then hung up and danced around the room.

"There is no wisdom, no insight, no plan that can succeed against the LORD." I didn't land my new teaching job by chance, coincidence, fate, or even the result of my own wisdom. It was God's plan.

Do you need to trust God's plan for you today?

REFLECTIONS: How has God worked His plan for you in specific ways throughout your marriage? Is there an area in which you need to trust Him right now?
PRAYER FOCUS: Thank God for the ways He has worked His plan for your lives in the past. Then tell Him that you trust Him for the future.

22
IRON SHARPENS IRON

As iron sharpens iron, so one man sharpens another.
PROVERBS 27:17

Has your partner ever said anything to you that challenged and irritated you at the same time? That happened to me many times in the first few years of our marriage. Naomi would say something that was right on, but since I didn't want to admit she was right, I felt less than receptive. But after a few years of marriage, it finally dawned on me: *This is the way it's supposed to be. This is good for me.*

God's Word says it this way: "As iron sharpens iron, so one man sharpens another." God uses our closest relationships to mold us. In the spirited interplay of two personalities, both lives are sharpened as each helps the other reflect deeply about words, actions, and ideas. This interaction produces something positive that wouldn't be there if it weren't for this vital interchange of heart and mind. In the process, lives are challenged and changed for the better.

There is no greater potential for applying this passage than in the marriage relationship, for no one has greater access to your life than your marriage partner. No one sees your ideas played out on the stage of life like the one you love. Therefore, no one has greater potential to help shape your ideas and thoughts—your very personality—than your spouse.

The scriptural image is a simple one: iron sharpening iron. A knife will come to a better edge only when it is sharpened against another piece of metal. Such sharpening is abrasive. It produces heat. It takes time. But in the end, it makes the edge sharper than it could have become any other way.

Iron sharpening iron—an appropriate image for the numerous

exchanges that happen over years of a loving marriage. You discuss ideas. You evaluate possible courses of action. You handle conflict. These processes can sometimes feel abrasive—can't they?—even in a loving relationship. Certainly they can generate a bit of heat. But in the long run, such interactions shape and mold and sharpen your lives. What an extraordinary opportunity for spiritual, psychological, and interpersonal growth.

Over the years, my wife has challenged me in the area of giving. She is naturally generous and giving, but I have to work at it. Naomi has been a holy irritant in my life, confronting me and forcing me to think through my motives. Through more than two decades of marriage, we've had numerous discussions about giving to someone in need or to a ministry we believe in. These conversations have forced me to examine my heart. I am a different person today because of her willingness to be "iron" in my life.

Next time you feel irritated over something your spouse says, stop and consider whether the Lord is actually using her to provide "sharpening" in your life. Learn to receive from her, to be challenged by her words. You'll find that the benefits are well worth the pain of the sharpening process.

REFLECTIONS: Identify some ways in which you've grown over the years because you've challenged each other. Tell each other how you're thankful for the "sharpening" such honesty has provided in your lives.

PRAYER FOCUS: Pray for a willingness to be sharpened by each other. Thank God for the positive effect you've had on each other's life.

23
WHEN IT'S GRAY

How can a young man keep his way pure?
By living according to your word.
PSALM 119:9

In a world that includes NC–17 movie ratings and same-sex marriages, you may sometimes feel confused about moral absolutes.
For Christian couples who live in a society that has jettisoned God's
values, the Psalmist provides a wonderful reminder: God's Word is
our standard, our yardstick for moral purity. God's Word, breathed
out for His children, must be our first and final authority when
making moral decisions.

The trouble is that some activities may seem gray, not black or
white. For example, where do you draw the line when it comes to
watching movies: "G," "PG-13," "R"? Is it wrong to buy a lotto
ticket? Is it wrong to allow our high-school children to attend a
school dance? Every Christian couple will have to answer these and
other questions as they build their home and decide on the values
they will live before their children.

As Naomi and I have navigated many moral conundrums,
we've generally put our final decisions through three biblical tests
that help us determine whether something is okay for us as a
couple:

*Test 1: Does the Bible have a clear command concerning this
action?* I'll never have to wonder if I can lie on my income tax
return or swear when I'm angry. The Bible has clear commands
about such things. I'm thankful that God has given many directives
which leave no doubt about the direction I should go. Sometimes,
making a decision is as simple as going to your concordance and
seeing what God says about the matter.

Test 2: Does the Bible have a principle that covers this action? A principle is a general truth that applies to many specific situations. For example, "You will reap what you sow" is a biblical principle. From this guideline, you can discern how to handle specific circumstances.

There is a wide range of issues in today's world that the Bible doesn't directly mention—everything from rap music to genetic engineering. Does that mean we can make up our own minds about these and other issues? Not exactly.

Just because the Bible doesn't mention something specifically doesn't mean a biblical principle doesn't apply to it. I had a friend in high school who tried to convince herself that marijuana was all right for her because the Bible doesn't specifically condemn it. While the Bible doesn't specifically mention this drug, Ephesians 5:18 contains a principle that applies: Don't get drunk. This principle would apply to getting high on *any* substance.

When the Bible doesn't give a clear command on a particular subject, couples must evaluate the subject according to biblical principles that might apply.

Test 3: Does the action offend my conscience? Your conscience is an important part of your moral compass. God has given it to you to help you know right from wrong. When the Holy Spirit came into your life, He began to use your conscience, sharpened by God's Word, to guide you (see 1 Timothy 1:19). At times, you may not be able to think of a biblical command or principle, but something deep inside says, "This is wrong." When your inner voice tells you this, heed it.

Couples will benefit as they handle moral issues directly, talking with each other, praying, and seeking God's wisdom. As you dialogue and examine God's Word together, I'm confident that you'll keep your way pure.

REFLECTIONS: Do you currently have a question about a moral issue that applies to you or your marriage? Is there a scriptural command or principle that might apply? What does your conscience say about the matter?

PRAYER FOCUS: Invite God to deepen your knowledge of His Word and to give you discernment to apply it. Ask Him to hone your conscience so you can make wise decisions about moral issues.

24
WE'RE JUST PASSING THROUGH

All these people were still living by faith when they died....
they admitted that they were aliens and strangers on earth.

HEBREWS 11:13

It's push-pull in this world we live in, isn't it? Undoubtedly you've felt the warmth of family and friends, the appreciation of God's creation, and the simple joys of life, such as reading a good book or enjoying a weekend away. Just as likely, you've experienced a painful loss or a difficult problem. While God's good gifts abound, troubles always lurk in the background. Life is a mixed bag.

The writer of Hebrews gives believers the key to living in such a world. As he lists the great heroes of the faith, the author helps us understand our status on this planet. He tells us that these heroes "admitted that they were aliens and strangers on earth." An alien is someone who is temporarily in residence. He lives every day in a country that is not his home. And that's how the writer of Hebrews wants believers to consider their status on this earth.

This idea is firmly rooted in the pages of God's Word. In Genesis 47:9, when Pharaoh asks Jacob his age, Jacob replies, "The years of my pilgrimage are a hundred and thirty." I like that: "the years of my pilgrimage." All of us are pilgrims in a strange land. This doesn't mean that we abandon the world we live in. In fact, those who do the most for this world are precisely the ones who think the most of the next. However, we can too easily allow either the joys of this world to distract us or the sorrows of this world to discourage us.

Many years ago, I heard a story that emphasized the importance of knowing our status on this earth. For his birthday, a certain king told his trusted advisor that he wanted a special gift. "If you are happy," the king said, "this gift will make you sad, and if you are sad, this gift will make you happy." The advisor was panic-stricken. How could he find such a gift? Where would he look?

For weeks, the advisor searched everywhere, scouring every shop, but he could find nothing that fit the king's description. The advisor beheld many fine gifts, but none fulfilled the king's request. On the king's birthday, the advisor went out one last time, feeling certain his search was futile. He found nothing and had sullenly turned toward home when he saw an old street vendor quietly selling wares. The advisor almost passed by but decided to take one last look. He told the street vendor what he wanted, and the old man smiled. "I have what you are looking for."

The king's advisor rushed to the palace with his gift and entered the throne room at the height of the joyous celebration. The servant presented his gift to the king. Smiling, the king opened the box and peered down at the present. It was a simple gold ring with these words inscribed on it: "This too shall pass." Instantly, the smile left the king's face as he realized that one day all the glory of his kingdom would be gone.

Believers, don't let either joys or sorrows cause you to forget that you're just passing through this world. Enjoy the good gifts that God provides. Trust Him in the midst of your difficulties. And always understand that "this too shall pass."

REFLECTIONS: What does it mean to live as an alien in this world? To live this way, would you have to make some changes in your life? in your marriage? If so, what changes would be warranted?
PRAYER FOCUS: Ask God for the ability to live with His perspective, that you might appreciate life's joys, endure life's sorrows, and keep your mind and heart set on your eternal home.

25
ACCEPTANCE IS THE SOIL OF CHANGE

Accept one another, then, just as Christ accepted you,
in order to bring praise to God.
ROMANS 15:7

Have you ever walked away from a conversation with each other more cognizant of your differences than your similarities? Have you become aware of an annoying habit or persistent weakness in your spouse that drives you crazy? Such discoveries aren't uncommon in a marriage relationship. Tension can mount in a marriage when differences begin to accumulate. At such times, you might wonder if your partner will ever change and what you can do to "help him along."

All kinds of strategies come to mind to change each other, don't they? Let me suggest one that may surprise you: acceptance. No matter how you try to help each other form new habits or break old ones, you run smack into an important relationship principle: Acceptance is the soil of change. Just as a living plant needs rich soil to grow, so a spouse grows only in the "soil" of his partner's genuine acceptance. No other medium will provide the environment for needed changes.

The basis for such acceptance is found in Paul's simple command to the Roman Christians. We must accept our marriage partners *as* Christ accepts us. How does Christ accept us? Unconditionally. No strings attached. Instead of condemning or judging us, He gives each one of us unconditional acceptance. Such love encourages us to respond to our Lord with love and obedience. His acceptance is the soil of daily change in our lives. In the same way, when we know that our partner doesn't look down on us or judge us, we're motivated to change.

I've certainly experienced this in my marriage. I'm an extrovert, no question about it. People energize me. I'm good at meeting people and engaging in small talk, and I have fun in groups. Naomi, on the other hand, is more subdued. She's great with people, too, but in a more gracious and gentle way. My sense of humor can get out of hand, and sometimes I can be spontaneous in a way that's uncomfortable for her.

This difference could have developed into a problem for us, but it hasn't. Why? Because Naomi accepts me. She communicates acceptance in her words, attitudes, and actions. Of course, she tells me when she's uncomfortable, and at those times, I try to make changes. I can do that because of her sure and certain acceptance. I know that she is for me, just as I am. Because this is true, I can admit my mistakes, knowing that she won't reject me.

Think about your own relationship. Does your attitude of acceptance free your partner to change? Can your spouse admit a mistake because he knows you'll still accept him? Does your relationship bring praise to God as people observe your ability to give and receive loving acceptance? Your answers to these questions and the ones below will help you evaluate whether your marriage affirms the simple principle that acceptance is the soil of change.

REFLECTIONS: When do you most appreciate your partner's acceptance? Tell him or her now. Do you ever feel disapproval or lack of acceptance? If so, when?

PRAYER FOCUS: Ask that Christ's attitude of acceptance would pervade your marriage and that you will experience the freedom such acceptance can bring.

26
BELIEVING THE BEST

Love…is ever ready to believe the best of every person.
1 CORINTHIANS 13:7 (AMPLIFIED)

Imagine for a moment that a wife hears her husband talk positively about her cooking to their dinner guests. She thinks, *Why is he talking about my cooking in front of these friends? He doesn't compliment my cooking much when we're alone. He just wants to look good in front of our friends.* Instead of feeling affirmed, she spends the evening feeling angry at her husband. She is cool to him after the guests leave, and he has no idea why.

What happened? This wife evaluated her husband's behavior negatively, choosing to believe that behind his good words were bad motives. In other words, she believed the worst about him. As a result, she felt angry.

Perhaps you've enacted a similar scenario in your own relationship at one time or another. Fortunately, the principle contained in 1 Corinthians 13:7 will help you avoid this and similar conflicts before they start. It's profoundly simple: Believe the best.

First Corinthians 13:7 doesn't equivocate much about this: Be willing, it says, to trust that your partner's behavior and motives are good ones. As you evaluate her words and actions, choose to give her the benefit of the doubt.

"Well," you say, "what if my spouse's motives aren't pure? What if my partner is being selfish or self-centered or thoughtless?" If your partner proves your good opinion wrong, you won't have lost a thing. If it becomes apparent that you need to talk further about a situation, then go for it. In the meantime, your positive evaluation gives your spouse the support and trust that any loving relationship demands.

Not too long ago, Naomi and I assembled a gas barbecue—you know, the kind you buy with "some assembly required." I've conceded over the years that Naomi is more mechanically minded than I, but I do have my pride. During this episode, I was dutifully working on assembling one part of the barbecue, and I was having some trouble. I asked for Naomi's input, but instead of giving me her opinion, she moved in, took away my wrench, and started working.

At that point, I had a choice. Either I would believe the best or the worst about Naomi's actions. If I believed the worst, my internal monologue would go something like this: *Man, she's taking control. Doesn't have any confidence in my abilities. This is the pits.* However, on this occasion, I chose to believe the best. I said to myself, *She's going further than I asked her to, but she's just trying to help me. That's okay.* It was that simple. The result, however, was enormous. Instead of harboring anger or speaking harsh words, I was able to thank her and go on.

Love believes the best. When love operates this way, a wonderful environment of safety develops within a relationship. Marriage partners don't have to live under such intense scrutiny when they can count on a positive evaluation of their words and actions. They avoid conflicts, enhance their intimacy, and foster safety within their relationship.

What about you? Have you been believing the best of each other? giving each other the benefit of the doubt? Why not make a commitment today to do that?

REFLECTIONS: Do you give each other the benefit of the doubt? Why not promise today to choose to believe the best about each other? If you've chosen to make that commitment, how can you follow through on it in the days to come?

PRAYER FOCUS: Pray for God's empowerment as you choose to monitor your thoughts about each other, giving each other the benefit of the doubt.

27
HONEST QUESTIONS

You are always righteous, O LORD, when I bring a case before you.
Yet I would speak with you about your justice: Why does the way
of the wicked prosper? Why do all the faithless live at ease?
JEREMIAH 12:1

Honest questions. I'm sure you have them from time to time, as do most believers. Life sometimes blurs our vision of God and His plan. When some injustice occurs or pain wreaks havoc in a loved one's life, honest questions arise.

Jeremiah 12:1 is about such a time. "God," Jeremiah says, "I have a question. What about all the people who choose to go their own way and do their own thing, yet their stock soars? They reject You, yet nothing seems to happen to them. In fact, if anything, they get richer. Why is that, O LORD?"

Jeremiah had a beef. He couldn't understand why wicked people prospered. It was an honest question. Because life is sometimes imponderable, honest questions are inevitable. Why do the wicked often prosper? Why do God's people sometimes suffer? Why do prayers offered in faith seem to go unanswered? Why this? Why now?

Recently, a situation occurred within my church family that was terribly difficult to understand. My friends Steve and Karolynn were on vacation in eastern Washington when Karolynn dropped to the ground, unconscious. This wonderful Christian couple were active in our church and loved by all. I had married them just eight months earlier in one of the most beautiful and touching ceremonies I've ever participated in. Just twenty-six years old, Karolynn died that day from a heart problem that no one had known existed.

Almost a year later, Steve continues to recover. When I talked with him last, he said, "I've never been angry at God. I'm hurt. I'm in pain. But I'm not angry. I'd like to know why God allowed this to happen. Somehow, though, God is going to help me. I know He loves me."

Steve doesn't understand the situation, but he has never doubted God's character. He has an honest question for God— "Why did You allow this in my life?"—but he asks it knowing that God loves him.

I think it's interesting that Jeremiah begins his question with a statement: "You are always righteous, O LORD." Jeremiah doesn't understand God's plan, but he *does* understand that God is righteous. Not once does he question his Father's character.

Sometimes knowing God's nature is all we have. The answers to our difficult questions elude us; the hard situations continue; the trials persist. But we know that we serve a good God and that we're never outside of His love. In the middle of life's storms, we hold on to our Father. Like Jeremiah, we return again and again to God's character: His love, His justice, His faithfulness. He will never change.

You may be in a situation that is hard for you to understand right now. If so, pour out your heart to God. Ask the hard, honest questions. Share your pain. But don't stop there. Meditate on God's character. Rest in His love. Trust Him until you have the answers to your questions.

REFLECTIONS: In what kinds of situations do you ask, "Why?" Has God answered you? Think of your marriage; have you learned to trust God together in the midst of difficulty?
PRAYER FOCUS: Ask for the ability to trust your Father's character in every situation. And if you presently face a difficult situation, ask God the hard, honest questions, affirming His good character all the while.

28
MAKE IT RIGHT

*So if you are about to offer your gift to God at the altar and
there you remember that your brother has something against you,
leave your gift there in front of the altar, go at once and make peace
with your brother, and then come back and offer your gift to God.*

MATTHEW 5:23–24 (TEV)

At some time in the next few days or weeks you'll probably offend
your marriage partner. You'll say an unkind word or forget a birthday or be insensitive to his needs. You'll have a silly argument,
selfishly insist on your own way, or embarrass him.

In other words, you'll blow it big time.

After you offend your spouse, you have to decide what to do
about it. You know as well as I do that when you offend your partner, your trespass hangs in the air like a black, ominous cloud. You
may close your eyes to it and try to avoid it, but it's there, and you
both know it.

When we were first married, I sometimes hurt Naomi and
was too proud to apologize. This would go on for hours, occasionally for a day, before I'd finally realize that our relationship would
suffer if I didn't swallow my pride and make things right. My
offense wouldn't just go away.

Interestingly, Jesus said something radical in this regard: If
someone has something against you, don't exercise the privilege of
worship before you make it right with that person. Don't walk—
run to restore that relationship! Echoing this principle, Paul later
said, "I strive always to keep my conscience clear before God and
man" (Acts 24:16).

A clear conscience means that you never offend another person
without making amends. If you're committed to a clear conscience,

you'll make things right between you and the one you've offended as soon as possible. Nowhere is this more important than in your marriage, where accumulated offenses can scuttle intimacy and sustain conflict.

So how do you make amends? First, let me suggest how *not* to do it. More than once, I've heard a husband or wife scowl a bit and say, "I'm sorry" or, even worse, "If I did something to offend you, I'm sorry." These responses don't do the job because they don't demonstrate a clear knowledge of the offense or exhibit sincere remorse for it. It's too easy to look down at the ground and mutter, "I'm sorry."

Instead, when you know that you don't have a clear conscience regarding your spouse, first determine how you offended him. Were you insensitive to his feelings? Did you speak harshly? Did you take control of a situation without regard for his desires? Discern the basic offense, and understand how it hurt your partner.

Then do something that's harder than almost anything else: Admit you were wrong. Look your partner in the eyes and say, "Honey, I was wrong for doing what I did. I want to know: Will you please forgive me?" Those words are so important for gaining a clear conscience. They make all the difference in the world.

The next time that dark cloud of offense hangs between you, don't ignore it. Believe me, it won't go away until you proactively do something about it. Do what Jesus commanded: Make it right.

REFLECTIONS: Do you keep a clear conscience with each other? Do you have one right now?
PRAYER FOCUS: Pray for a soft heart that can admit wrong. Ask God to help you keep a clear conscience with each other.

29
THE POWER OF WORDS

*Do not let any unwholesome talk come out of your mouths, but only
what is helpful for building others up according to their needs,
that it may benefit those who listen.*

EPHESIANS 4:29

You've both experienced it, haven't you? The power of words. Can
you think of a time you were out of sorts and a compliment or word
of appreciation from your spouse sent your spirits soaring? You're
familiar, too, with words that tear down. They can bite into your
psyche like an enraged pit bull clinging to a helpless victim.

Ephesians 4:29 not only warns us to *stop* using words that tear
down, it also counsels us to *start* speaking words that build up.
Applied to marriage, it offers a simple prescription: Discern what
your spouse needs at the moment, and speak a word that will meet
that need emotionally and spiritually.

Two common situations stand out in which your partner especially needs words that build:

1. When your spouse has made a mistake. Every one of us makes
mistakes. Guess who has a fabulous ringside seat from which to
observe those mistakes? You guessed it: your marriage partner. No
one is in a better position to see firsthand how you really messed
up...or has a greater opportunity to speak comforting words.

Not long ago, my pickup truck wouldn't start. My wife asked
me if the battery was dead, and I told her that it couldn't be because
I hadn't left the lights on. I had the pickup towed away; that cost
me forty dollars. Then the mechanic made his diagnosis: The battery was dead. Someone had left the dome light on. The mechanic's
diagnosis cost me another forty dollars. Bottom line: eighty dollars
for a battery recharge.

Here's what my wife said to me about this costly mistake: "I understand, Art. It's not always easy to know what's wrong with a car." She could have made me pay emotionally for my mistake. Instead, she spoke words that built me up. Instead of a drain, I received an emotional boost from her words.

2. *When your spouse is discouraged.* Life will inevitably provide circumstances that lead to potential discouragement. Your job doesn't progress as fast as you'd like; your face begins to develop a road map of wrinkles. Sometimes failure will discourage us, and this can be one of the greatest points of need in all of our lives, a time of great vulnerability.

There are no magic formulas for dispelling discouragement. Sometimes it's just a matter of time and prayer. However, an encouraging word can uplift your partner as he works through the situation. Words of affirmation or a cogent reminder of God's truth can make all the difference. They meet the need of the moment, helping lift your spouse's spirits as he senses your support.

When I see that my wife is discouraged, I try to speak words of love to her. I may not be able to solve the problem, but I can assure her that she is loved. When I feel discouraged, Naomi often reminds me that God is pleased with me apart from my performance; these words of encouragement help me keep perspective.

Put the power of words to work in your own marriage. Be the one who builds up your partner at his point of need. Let discouragement or failure elicit words that benefit your spouse. Then stand back and watch the effect of your words.

REFLECTIONS: What situation makes you feel most vulnerable and in need of uplifting words? What words of encouragement do you most appreciate?

PRAYER FOCUS: Ask God for the ability to discern your partner's need for encouragement and for the wisdom to speak words that will build up your spouse.

30
CHOICES

*You were taught, with regard to your former way of life, to
put off your old self....and to put on the new self, created to be like
God in true righteousness and holiness.*

EPHESIANS 4:22, 24

Do you sometimes feel discouraged in your spiritual journey? As individuals and as a couple, you want to progress, but you don't always see the changes you'd like. What's the key to positive change?

C. S. Lewis offers some insightful and challenging words:

> Someone who is not a good tennis player may now and then make a good shot. What you mean by a good player is the man whose eye and muscles and nerves have been so trained by making innumerable good shots that they can now be relied on.... In the same way a man who perseveres in just actions gets in the end a certain quality of character.... Every time you make a choice you are turning the central part of you, the part of you that chooses, into something a little different from what it was before.[1]

What Lewis describes is choice. All of us must make a series of choices every day: how we will spend our time, how we will respond to adversity, how we will speak to people at home or at work. We make innumerable choices day in and day out, and the accumulation of those choices changes us. Like a tennis player who perseveres in practicing effective shots and thus gains a consistent tennis game, each believer who perseveres in making the right moral and spiritual choices gains a consistent Christian walk. Eventually, your choices result in Christ's character residing in you.

Ephesians 4:22, 24 says it this way: "Put off your old self....put on the new self." In other words, choose to say no to the actions consistent with the old self's behavior and choose to say yes to actions consistent with God's righteous character. When you make those choices consistently, you become more and more like Jesus.

As simple as it sounds, positive change boils down to choices. Becoming Christlike is a process, and your choices determine how quickly you'll progress. It's no good saying things such as "Hey, that's the way I'm wired. I just blow up when I'm angry." You may have learned an explosive response to anger-provoking situations, but you had a hand in the "wiring." You can unlearn that response and relearn a more effective, Christlike one. That's what "putting off" and "putting on" mean.

The bottom line: God created us with the ability to change. In fact, He expects us to change year in and year out. What does it take? Consistently good choices such as reading our Bibles, choosing to serve our spouses, controlling our thinking, praying when we're tempted. When we make good choices over and over again, God changes our character.

Now think a moment about those areas that seem so resistant to change in your life or marriage. What choices are you making? Are you willing to persevere in doing the right thing, even when it hurts? What choices can you make this day that will honor God and bring you closer to Him?

REFLECTIONS: If you feel safe enough, share with each other areas resistant to change. Listen to each other without giving solutions.
PRAYER FOCUS: Pray for each other in the areas you just discussed. Invite God to change your character by helping you both make consistently good choices in those challenging areas.

31
LIVING FOR WHAT LASTS

*Then he said to them, "Watch out! Be on your guard against
all kinds of greed; a man's life does not consist in the
abundance of his possessions."*

LUKE 12:15

If you're doing this devotional together, more than likely you are
both believers. You know that possessions are *not* the most important thing in life. Most of the time, you can probably resist a
materialistic mind-set, escaping the magnetic pull of the shopping
malls and the less subtle temptation of the latest mail-order catalog.
You know, or at least suspect, that materialism is not good.

But as Americans, we can easily get caught up in the rush to
accumulate goods and the desire for more and more—the bigger
house, the new car, the better vacation. A glimpse of your neighbor's new luxury car shining brightly in the sun or a conversation
about a neighbor's recent Florida vacation can get you to thinking,
"If we just had a little more…" If you don't watch yourself, you can
begin measuring your progress by the newness of your furniture or
your ability to afford a big-screen TV. Such thoughts can squeeze
satisfaction out of your lives bit by bit.

That's why Jesus boldly declared to believers: "Watch out! Be
on your guard against all kinds of greed; a man's life does not consist in the abundance of his possessions." Simply put, live for what
lasts. Find out what is of eternal significance, Christ says, and put
your energy and heart into that. Quick tip: Possessions aren't on the
"most important" list. Jesus' warning is a stark reminder of how
alluring our possessions can be yet how devoid of ultimate value
they truly are.

Of course, Jesus didn't say that possessions are evil or that ownership is wrong. For example, in many cases it is wise to own a home. Christ doesn't forbid working hard and realizing the benefits of our income. But we must realize that possessions are shadows, not reality. Therefore, our most important goals should focus on matters of eternal significance, such as family, character, service, and a personal relationship with God.

When we focus on possessions, we discover that a feeling of dissatisfaction begins to dog our lives. As soon as we obtain one object, our hearts set their affections on the next prize, with little enjoyment of what God has already provided. We forget about what God has already given us and focus on what we lack. We make more but enjoy it less. Inevitably, this begins to affect our marriage.

Over the years, I've observed that the most contented couples are those who live for what lasts. They may or may not own a home; they may or may not drive a new car. But they do put their time into relationships with God, family, and others. Such couples constantly encourage my wife and me to be satisfied with what we have and to live for what lasts.

If you find that your satisfaction with life is at a low ebb, you may be measuring your life in terms of your possessions. It's wise, I think, for couples to periodically take a reality check in this area and ask some hard questions. Why not spend a moment now to do just that?

REFLECTIONS: What first comes to mind about your own life when you read Jesus' words: "a man's life does not consist in the abundance of his possessions"? How does this principle work in your life? in your marriage? What are your priorities as a couple? Do your relationships with God and with each other come first? Are you living for what lasts?

PRAYER FOCUS: Ask God to help you value what is most important and to help you choose priorities of eternal significance.

32
OUR CALENDARS

There is a time for everything, and a season
for every activity under heaven.
ECCLESIASTES 3:1

When was the last time you heard yourself ask, "Where does the time go?" If you're like me, you probably said it not too long ago. We all seem to barrel ahead in the high-speed race of life, barely able to stop to catch our breath.

As a married couple, you'll find it beneficial to discuss with each other how you handle your time. To stay in sync regarding your priorities, I encourage you to seek God's wisdom as you make time-management decisions together. Three Scripture passages provide important and practical help:

1. Use time strategically. Proverbs 24:27 outlines a cryptic but important concept: "Finish your outdoor work and get your fields ready; after that, build your house." King Solomon used an agricultural example to make his point. In that economy, getting the fields ready for planting was the most important job. This verse exhorts us to put first things first, to prioritize our time and attack our most important tasks before anything else.

The bottom line: Set priorities. Know what's important. Remember that when people don't know their priorities they empower others to shape their lives. Couples can benefit by sitting down and discussing what comes first in their lives, what's most important to them as a couple. Successful Christian couples I know make God and family their top two priorities.

2. Use time carefully. Ephesians 5:15-16 makes this point: "Therefore be careful how you walk, not as unwise men, but as wise, making the most of your time...." (NASB). Couples can make the most of their time when they plan carefully. Such planning flows from priorities and is bathed in prayer.

Whenever my wife and I spend a weekend away, we try to take our calendars with us and plan our schedule for the upcoming months, keeping in mind what's most important. We try to set aside time for family days and future weekends away. We pray, asking God to help us know His will.

Your marriage may benefit from a schedule-planning weekend. If you can't get away to do it, how about taking a long Saturday morning breakfast at a nearby restaurant to plan the upcoming quarter?

3. *Use time humbly.* James speaks eloquently here: "Why, you do not even know what will happen tomorrow. What is your life? You are a mist that appears for a little while and then vanishes. Instead, you ought to say, 'If it is the Lord's will, we will live and do this or that'" (James 4:14–15). This passage isn't meant to depress you! But it does make a simple point: We must realize that every breath we take is a gift from God. We ought to joyfully receive each moment and prayerfully make the most of the time God gives us. Using time humbly means recognizing our human frailty and making sure that we spend time in a way that honors God.

Look back through the pages of last year's calendar and think of all the hours they represent. For a moment, hold your year in your hands. Then take your current calendar and flip through the next several months, seeing them stretch out before you with infinite possibilities. Together, commit those possibilities to God and ask Him to help you use time strategically, carefully, and humbly.

REFLECTIONS: What can you do today to ensure that you use time strategically, carefully, and humbly? Would you be willing to schedule a planning time together to help you in this area?

PRAYER FOCUS: Invite God to help you prioritize and plan your time in a way that reflects His priorities.

33
PROBLEM OR INCONVENIENCE?

Be joyful always; pray continually;
give thanks in all circumstances.

1 THESSALONIANS 5:16–18

Have you ever had one of those weeks when nothing goes right? As you try to work through the difficulties, you find yourself growing more and more morose. Soon, you're in a serious Bad Mood.

A few years ago, I read a true story that has helped me keep God's perspective at such times and follow His command to "give thanks in all circumstances."

In 1959, a young man named Robert Fulghum got a night-clerk job at a resort in northern California. His boss had bleak views of employee care. Throughout his first week on the job, the boss fed the young man and each of his fellow employees two wieners, sauerkraut, and stale rolls every day, then had the audacity to deduct the price of the meals from their wages.

Finally, the young man blew up in front of his fellow clerk, Sigmund Wollman. He yelled and complained for twenty minutes nonstop while his colleague sat, unblinking, before him. Finally his fellow clerk spoke to him. Sigmund was a Jew who had survived the Auschwitz concentration camp during World War II. This is what Sigmund told the young man:

> Lissen, Fulghum. Lissen me, lissen me. You know what's wrong with you? It's not wieners and kraut and it's not the boss and it's not the chef and it's not this job…. Fulghum, you think you know everything, but you don't know the difference between an inconvenience and a problem. If you break your neck, if you have nothing to eat, if your

house is on fire—then you got a problem. Everything else is inconvenience. Life *is* inconvenient. Life is lumpy. Learn to separate the inconveniences from the real problems. You will live longer. And will not annoy people like me so much. Good night.[1]

Problem or inconvenience? Not a bad way to view the twists and turns of life. When viewed from God's perspective, most of life's difficulties would probably come down squarely in the inconvenience camp.

Keeping God's perspective—that's the key, isn't it?

That was true for me recently. My computer decided to shut down in the middle of the day. Since most days I spend a good deal of time using my computer, this was a major interruption. After two hours, I was beginning to feel irked at the delay in my work. Just about the time I was heading for a Bad Mood, Wollman's question popped into my mind: Is this a problem or an inconvenience? After thinking about it, I definitely had to categorize it as an inconvenience. Irritating, yes; of major consequence, no.

As I sat at my desk that day, I reflected how easily we allow little things to snatch away our joy. Seeing difficulties from God's perspective is the antidote. Problems look a lot smaller in light of His power and presence. That's why 1 Thessalonians 5:16–18 can say: "Be joyful always; pray continually; give thanks in all circumstances." With His help, we can choose joy through every inconvenience, prayer through every problem, and thanksgiving through all of life, knowing that God travels with us on life's journey.

What about you? Have you been stressed out recently? If so, perhaps you've elevated an inconvenience to the status of a problem. The counsel of God's Word? See your difficulty from God's perspective, then thank Him that He's with you in whatever circumstances you face.

REFLECTIONS: Are you currently facing a difficulty in your life?

Are you keeping God's perspective about it? Is it a real problem or truly just an inconvenience?

PRAYER FOCUS: Pray for God's perspective during life's difficulties and for His strength and joy as you work through them.

34
LOVING YOUR SPOUSE
WITHOUT LOSING
YOURSELF

*Each of you should look not only to your own interests, but
also to the interests of others. Your attitude should
be the same as that of Christ Jesus.*

PHILIPPIANS 2:4–5

Think about your dating years for a moment. Wives, do you remember going to those monster-truck shows, trying your best to enjoy them? Do you remember going with him to all those action-adventure movies that lulled you into a comatose-like state? Husbands, do you remember driving fifty miles with her to see the local tulip festival, all the while dreaming of the softball game you were missing? You did things you'd never do on your own, all because you loved each other. You wanted to give; you wanted to sacrifice. It's usually not until the honeymoon is over that couples begin to ask, "How do I give to my spouse without being taken advantage of? How do I choose to serve without being overpowered?" In other words, "How do I love my spouse without losing myself?"

I believe that couples can make two choices that help them keep this balance. First, husbands and wives need to recognize their own needs and set limits when appropriate. Second, husbands and wives need to choose to serve their spouses regardless of return.

"What?" you ask. "Recognize my own needs? Set limits? That doesn't sound very Christlike." Read Philippians 2:4–5 again. This passage recognizes that you have interests. If within your marriage those needs and desires constantly take a backseat to your spouse's, you will eventually feel used and discouraged.

If one of you always pleases and the other always controls, you have neither a satisfying marriage nor a Christlike relationship. If you don't set limits, your partner will fail to give you something vital to a good relationship: respect.

Setting limits simply means saying, "This is what I need; this is where I stand." For example, if your husband says, "I'm going to the gym to work out. See you at supper," you might reply, "Honey, that doesn't work for me. Let me share my schedule with you." What did you just do? You set a limit.

As you set limits, however, you must also choose to serve your spouse. A servant attitude is imperative to adopting Christ's character and vital to every marriage relationship. We're called to look out for our partner's interests, even to put those interests above our own when love dictates.

This happens in small ways all the time. "Here's a cup of coffee, hon" or "I'll take care of the dishes tonight. You go relax." A servant attitude pushes out into the deep waters of sacrifice on a daily basis. Like the time you pick up his socks for the millionth time. Like the time you take care of the kids so she can take a class she's interested in. Self-denial is part of the marital journey.

You might ask, "How can you serve and set limits at the same time?" The balance is found in *how* you serve. If you feel *forced* to give, if you can't set limits, then service is slavery. If, however, you *choose* to give, then service is a healthy expression of love. Jesus is our prime example. He didn't have his life taken from Him—He gave it. Like Christ, husbands and wives must choose to lay down their lives for their partners.

Do you need to set a limit today? Do you need to choose to sacrifice? The balance sometimes brings tension, but healthy couples know how to love their spouses without losing themselves.

REFLECTIONS: As a couple, how are you doing in this area? Do you both consistently set limits *and* choose to serve? Or does one of you have a tendency to please and the other to control? If it's the latter, what can you do to better balance your relationship?

PRAYER FOCUS: Pray for a servant attitude toward each other as well as the ability to understand and express your own needs.

35
HANDLING ANGER

*"In your anger do not sin": Do not let the sun go down while you
are still angry, and do not give the devil a foothold.*

EPHESIANS 4:26–27

Make no mistake, you *do* get angry at your partner. All spouses do.
Some more, some less. You may call it irritation or frustration, but
the bottom line is that you feel the hard knot of anger churning in
the pit of your stomach. So what happens in your marriage when
one of you feels angry with the other?

Ephesians 4:26–27 doesn't condemn all anger. It does, however, say that we must handle anger constructively. According to
this passage, when you fail to handle anger effectively, you actually
give the devil a foothold in your life and, I might add, your marriage. You give the evil one a place to inject his poison into your
relationship. His venom—bitterness, rage, unforgiveness, misunderstanding, distance—begins to filter into each interaction.

We can be grateful that God has given us a two-part prescription for preventing such infection: (1) Stay in control,
communicating your anger directly; and (2) take care of your anger
quickly, never sustaining it. When you employ these two strategies,
you'll handle your anger effectively.

This passage says, "In your anger do not sin," acknowledging
that you *will* feel angry sometimes but asserting that when you are
angry, you can stay in control. Anger doesn't have to lead to sin.

But—let's be honest—sometimes it does. Couples sometimes
demonstrate their anger by criticizing or yelling or slamming doors
or withdrawing...you name it! A *demonstration* of anger usually
means that you're communicating your anger indirectly in a way
that will hurt your partner. Certainly, such venting of anger will
damage the relationship.

What's the alternative? Instead of *demonstrating* anger, *communicate* it. Talk about your anger directly; express why you've become angry. When you communicate your anger directly, your partner can hear what you're saying. Communicating anger is an act of self-control that ensures you do no harm to the relationship while helping your spouse understand your pain.

Let's say, for example, that your wife makes a dinner engagement without consulting you first. You feel irritated about it. You don't want to hurt her, but you need to discuss it. How do you start the conversation? How about this: "Honey, I understand that you want some time with the Wilsons, but when you schedule a dinner without consulting me, I feel bypassed. I guess I feel irritated about it. Could we talk?"

Ephesians 4:26–27 gives us another tip for handling anger: Take care of your anger quickly. The passage says it this way: "Do not let the sun go down while you are still angry." In other words, don't allow your anger to fester. Don't feed your anger, sustaining it over days or weeks. Even if you can't solve the problem quickly, let go of the anger. Forgive your partner. Anything less will allow walls to build between you and your spouse.

Today or tomorrow, your spouse may do something that brings the hot flush of anger to the surface. Annoyance, aggravation, and irritation arise even in the best of marriages. Remember at such times that, with God's help, you can successfully handle your anger.

REFLECTIONS: How do you usually react when you feel angry? As a couple, how can you improve your ability to handle anger?
PRAYER FOCUS: Pray for God's presence and power in your relationship, helping you recognize your anger and handle it well.

36
MAXIMUM LOAD LIMIT

But God keeps his promise, and he will not allow you to be tested
beyond your power to remain firm; at the time you are put
to the test, he will give you the strength to endure it,
and so provide you with a way out.

1 CORINTHIANS 10:13 (TEV)

Have you felt the weight of life pressing on you lately? Between family life, jobs, and church activities, maybe you're feeling overwhelmed. Or perhaps you're in the middle of a difficult situation that challenges every inner resource you possess. You might wonder, *Will I make it through this one?*

For fifteen years, my father drove a large tractor-trailer rig down the highway for a living. As he drove, he was required to stop at weigh stations along the freeway. He disliked the task, but he knew it had to be done. Each truck has a "maximum load limit," a weight it's not allowed to exceed, and the weigh stations check this.

Apparently, there's a good reason for such limits. Our national highway system is designed to bear only so much weight. If truck drivers habitually carry more weight over it, our roads will crack and crumble, deteriorating under the excessive load.

In the same way, God understands how much weight each of His children can carry. When He allows trials to enter our lives, He knows our maximum load limit and doesn't allow more of a burden than we can bear. He may not take us *out* of the situation, but He always will give us what we need to persevere *through* the difficulties.

My wife and I have had to learn this principle because we've weathered crises, transitions, changes, and even some tragedies together. These challenges have come in all shapes and sizes. We faced a crisis many years ago that took us close to the edge. I had just started seminary and had no employment. Our money was running short, and there seemed no way out. Stress? You'd better believe it!

Naomi and I knew that God would take care of us, that He wouldn't ask more of us than we could handle. But what we *knew* and what we *felt* didn't always match! We didn't feel we could handle the challenge placed before us. However, we joined in prayer every day, asking God to help, guide, and empower us. We knew God had our load limit in mind. And He faithfully provided! He supplied an odd job here and an odd job there until I snagged steady employment. In the meantime, He gave us what we needed to stay connected to Him and to each other.

At times you may have wondered if things in your life could get any worse. You may have felt that you'd reached your load limit and that God had taken you to the very edge of your ability to cope. If you see your life careening out of control, hang onto the truth of 1 Corinthians 10:13. God will not allow you to carry a heavier load than you can bear. Period.

REFLECTIONS: Name a time you felt you had reached your limit. How did God intervene? Are you facing anything right now that seems overwhelming?

PRAYER FOCUS: Ask God for the ability to trust Him in the middle of your difficulties, for help in any current problems you face, and for peace as He works in you.

37
FITTING TOGETHER

And "fit in with" each other, because of your
common reverence for Christ.

EPHESIANS 5:21 (PHILLIPS)

During the beginning weeks and months of our marital dance, every move was unfamiliar. One by one, Naomi and I created the steps together. Who would pay the bills? What church would we attend? Who would take the first shower of the day? How would we make decisions? What would we do with our free time?

We had to accommodate, adapt, adjust. This process boiled down to recognizing our differing wants, needs, and perspectives and choosing to work with those differences. We learned the give and take of married life in those early years, and we're still working on it twenty-two years later.

In your own marriage, you each have different gifts and strengths. Choosing to "fit in" means receiving the benefits of those strengths and the unique perspective that goes with them. Perhaps one of you has an artistic flair while the other can organize anything anywhere. Perhaps one of you likes moonlit walks while the other prefers mountain biking at dawn. If you respect those and other differences and commit yourselves to making room for them in your relationship, you'll enrich your lives and strengthen your marriage.

My wife likes to balance the checkbook. She finds satisfaction in it. I, on the other hand, never once balanced my checkbook before marrying her. It would be pretty dumb for me to insist on handling our finances when I'm hooked up to a lady who is not only good at it but (hard for me to believe) *likes* it. Fitting in with Naomi has meant affirming that strength and following her lead with our budget.

One problem with fitting in is that differences create a push-pull in the relationship. Since each of you has a different perspective, some sparks will occasionally fly. Inevitably, you may sometimes feel that the puzzle pieces of your personalities just don't fit together.

When fitting in seems especially hard, make sure you do three things. First, *communicate regularly.* Try to see the issue from each other's perspective. Really listen to each other, and check to ensure you understand what your partner says. Second, *pray together.* When you're having trouble, invite God to bring you unity. Whether you're trying to make a decision or learning to cooperate on a project, you need God's help. Ask Him for it. Finally, *compromise when necessary.* All marriages sometimes require respectful compromise. There are many roads leading to the same destination. Just because your spouse doesn't travel on your road, that doesn't mean he's not headed in the right direction. Choose to support your spouse, and compromise for the good of your relationship.

Working through these differences can cause tension, but don't give up. Christian marriage partners just can't afford to cop out on the process. Why? Because our motivation for fitting in with each other is our mutual reverence and respect for Jesus. As Ephesians 5:21 says, if you love and respect Jesus, then you'll learn to fit in with each other. There is no wiggle room here; fitting in glorifies God.

Have you recently experienced some frustration as you try to blend your lives together? Keep persevering, and allow your common reverence for Christ to motivate and encourage you.

REFLECTIONS: Talk about one or two ways you're different from each other. How do you deal with those differences? Are there areas in which you need to accommodate, adapt, or adjust right now? If so, how can you do so?

PRAYER FOCUS: Thank God for your partner's unique strengths and perspective. Invite God to bring unity as you learn to accommodate each other.

38
THE POWER OF A GOAL

So we make it our goal to please him.

2 CORINTHIANS 5:9

Tiger Woods, the young man who won the prestigious Masters Golf Tournament in his rookie year, is a clear example of a man with a goal. What is it? To be the best golfer on the face of the planet. That goal has focused his life, funneling his energy in one dynamic direction. The result? He's the youngest man in history to win the Masters. How's that for the power of a goal?

Since goals channel our efforts and focus our activities, believers benefit from spiritual goals. In 2 Corinthians, Paul declared a goal so foundational that it penetrated every facet of his life. The goal? To please God. Essentially, Paul says in 2 Corinthians 5:9, "My life goal is to sift every decision, every action, every thought through one simple filter: Does it please my God?"

This goal powerfully affected his direction in life. From that dusty Damascus road to a cold Roman prison cell, Paul's decision to please the Lord focused his life to an extraordinary degree. In the pages of Scripture, we see him making decisions with that one thought in mind. He put shoe leather to his goal again and again.

What hinders *us* from pursuing this goal? Why is pleasing the Lord sometimes the last thing on our minds? We could answer this question in a variety of ways, some simple and others complex. One important answer, however, is this: We fail to keep our goal continually in our minds.

You see, nothing remains automatically alive in our minds and hearts. Your goal to please Him is no exception. That goal must be remembered, fed, nourished, and pursued. Believers need reminders every day of what's most important. That's one of the reasons a daily "quiet time" is so important. Daily Bible reading and prayer remind you of Whose you are, Whom you serve, and ultimately of your goal to please Him.

Tiger Woods is a good example of a man who keeps his goal alive. When he was a little boy, he would fall asleep at night memorizing the golf scores of greats like Jack Nicklaus and Arnold Palmer. What was he doing? Remembering his goal, nourishing his dream, keeping his goal alive in his mind and heart.

What about you? Are you wandering spiritually a bit these days? finding it difficult to focus? Maybe you need to remember Paul's bottom line: "So we make it our goal to please him." If you'll take time each day to remind yourself of this priority and ask His help in fulfilling it, perhaps with Paul you'll experience the tremendous power of a goal.

REFLECTIONS: Share with each other where you are spiritually. Have you nourished your goal of pleasing God? If so, how? What would it take to keep this goal alive in your heart during the next week? Can you help each other do so?

PRAYER FOCUS: Pray for a greater awareness of God's presence throughout the day. Ask for His help in knowing His will and learning to please Him.

39
WEAR SHOES YOU
WANT FILLED

Follow my example, as I follow the example of Christ.
1 CORINTHIANS 11:1

Has the impact of the parenting task hit you between the eyes recently? You may wonder how you will achieve maximum influence in your child's life. How will you teach your child morals, spiritual values, love for God? Have you felt the full force of this responsibility, the enormity of the job?

Paul must have felt similar emotions as he "fathered" the churches God had placed in his care. There was so much these new Christians needed to know! So many needs! *How will I ever "parent" the church to maturity?* he must have wondered. Certainly Paul gave his spiritual children the teaching they needed. But as he led them toward Christ, he understood one critical principle: You often teach best by example. Paul challenged his spiritual kids, "Follow my example, as I follow the example of Christ." He knew that his example could have tremendous power to guide them toward maturity.

We can apply this principle to parenting by wearing shoes that we want filled. Our children will learn as much from watching our example as they will from any formal teaching we give them. When we understand and apply this principle, the enormous task of parenting seems much less daunting. What's in our hearts is translated into action, and our kids have ringside seats to observe our behavior. Believe me, they do watch us, and our example has tremendous power to influence their lives.

I remember a woman who became a Christian a few years ago. She attended the church I pastor, and I baptized her not long after she accepted Christ. This woman brought her six-year-old girl with her to the baptism. As they drove home that day, the little girl said, "Jesus has a secret."

"What's that, honey?" her mother asked.

"The Lord is very happy with you," said the little girl.

Our children are watching!

What do your kids hear when someone cuts you off in traffic? What do they observe when you discover that the recent rainstorm has deposited six inches of water in your basement? Do they see you pray and read your Bible regularly? Kids are great observers. We teach our children so much by the values we live out day after day.

"What about mistakes?" you ask. No problem. Kids understand mistakes. If a mom loses her temper but then seeks forgiveness, her child will almost always freely forgive. Of course, if screaming is the norm, and if apologies are given but consistently forgotten, this pattern affects a child's view of his or her parents. What's more, these parents won't retain as much influence over their child. Honest mistakes, however, can actually become teaching points as children see their parents admit mistakes and change their behavior.

Bottom line? Wear shoes you want filled. Being a good parent has a lot to do with being a good example. When the parenting task seems too big to handle, realize that your consistent example of honoring God in word, action, and attitude will make a world of difference in your child's life.

REFLECTIONS: Affirm each other by sharing the specific ways in which you both provide good examples for your children. Now discuss one way you could improve the example your children observe each day.

PRAYER FOCUS: Ask God to help you be good examples for your children and for wisdom in the parenting task.

40
LASTING LOVE

*"Haven't you read... 'For this reason a man will leave his father and
mother and be united to his wife, and the two will become one
flesh'? So they are no longer two, but one. Therefore what
God has joined together, let man not separate."*

MATTHEW 19:4–6

Ken and Dora Nickel, my wife's parents, stand smiling as they prepare to leave. They're dressed in their Sunday best. Everything
shines, including their faces. They're happy at the prospect of this
Sunday afternoon.

Forty years together—definitely worth a celebration. Members
of their church congregation, family, and friends have been invited
to recognize with them the value of commitment, the miracle of
married love, and the wonder of God's "joining" so many years ago.

We're going to the church's fellowship hall early to make last-
minute preparations. Naomi and I are looking at the picture
collage one more time. Forty years of memories, the earliest pictures in black and white, are carefully mounted on two colored
squares of poster board. Ken and Dora's wedding photo is in the
center. Dad stands tall and serious in a dark suit; Mom gazes out
with a serene smile of contented joy. Other photos surround that
one, capturing both the milestones and the common scenes of
everyday life—two people working out God's joining, learning to
love and to live together.

A little later, we arrive at the church, and people begin to
trickle in for the open house. Old friends shake hands and hug, and
Mom and Dad tell stories of their life together. People gather
around the collage and cluck and smile and wonder. "They look so
young," these friends and family members say. "Weren't they a

handsome couple?" "Now what year was Naomi born?"

Later on, after most people have arrived, we gather together for a short program. Naomi and I sing "Cherish the Treasure." I can see Mom dab her eyes as she listens to the music and remembers her wedding day. Dad puts his arm around her shoulders.

Their pastor, a friend for many years, stands and speaks eloquently about their life together. He tells of their marital journey, the joys and sorrows of forty years together. He talks about the importance of their commitment to each other, and how that commitment has anchored their relationship. Year after year, they've clung to God and to each other, forging the strongest of bonds, growing a relationship resistant to the forces that have threatened to separate them. Though God has joined Ken and Dora, he says, they have nurtured that precious gift for the last forty years. In the audience, we nod as we listen. We drink in the words, knowing them to be true and good and wise.

Later, we clean up, loading the pictures, flowers, and leftover cake into the car. We walk out of the church with Naomi's parents. We're all thinking the same thing: How good is God's plan for uniting a man and a woman! How rare the joy of married love. How right to affirm a treasure so precious.

REFLECTIONS: Reflect on your thoughts about your marriage by sharing your answers to these questions:
1. The joys we experience because of our commitment to each other are…
2. Something that has recently threatened to separate us is…
3. A way we can overcome that separation and honor God's joining is…
4. When I think about the future with you, I most look forward to…

PRAYER FOCUS: Pray for a deepening of your relationship. Ask God to help you make decisions that will keep your marriage strong and growing.

41
FINDING YOUR TRUE SELF

If anyone would come after me, he must deny himself and take up
his cross daily and follow me. For whoever wants to save his life
will lose it, but whoever loses his life for me will save it.

LUKE 9:23–24

Life can feel so empty sometimes. You have everything you need, including Christ in your life, yet you feel that something is missing. At such times, Luke 9:23–24 may hold the answer to the barren feeling in your heart.

Do you see the paradox in these verses? "Following me," Jesus says, "means denial, losing ultimate control of your life. However, in giving your life, you end up finding your true self." Our Lord expects us to live lives of self-denial as we follow Him, but in doing so, we gain far more than we give.

I don't want you to get the wrong idea about Jesus' words. "Deny yourself" isn't a call to some ascetic lifestyle in which the worse you treat yourself, the closer you come to God. Heaven forbid! "Deny yourself" is simply our Lord's declaration that the Christian life should be Christ-centered, not self-centered. We shouldn't do our own bidding; we should do Christ's.

In his novel *The Silver Chair,* C. S. Lewis aptly depicts the struggle to follow Jesus despite the cost. In this book, Aslan (who symbolizes Jesus) gives the other central characters specific instructions to follow. His last instruction is very difficult and might result in death. Yet one of the characters urges the others on, saying, "Whether we die or not, we will have the satisfaction of doing what Aslan has told us."[1]

Lewis hints at an important idea: A believer gains ultimate satisfaction only by obeying Christ. Paradoxically, as we sacrifice our will for His, He brings fulfillment into our lives. Joy is a by-product of loving God and others. Seek happiness through self-fulfillment, and you'll miss it every time. Sacrifice your own agenda to serve Christ and others, and joyous fulfillment is assured. "Whoever loses his life for me will save it," Jesus said. *The Message* puts it this way: "Self-sacrifice is the way, my way, to finding yourself, your true self." Finding your true self happens only in the refining fire of self-sacrifice. Your decision to speak a kind word, to maintain a positive attitude, to help someone in need, to stay committed to a difficult relationship will all require sacrifice. But these decisions also produce character. They teach us reliance on our Lord and release in us the joy of obeying Him.

When Naomi and I talk about our life in Christ, we know something is wrong when we feel that life is dull. Instead of looking for amusements to distract us, we're learning to pull close to Christ and seek to obey His voice. We ask, "What do You want for our lives, Lord? What is Your next step for us?" At such times, we ask God to bring us back to center, to show us what it means to sacrifice our will for His. As a result, we experience individual and marital renewal.

What about you? Does life seem a bit dull right now? If so, return to center with Jesus' words: "Self-sacrifice is the way, my way, to finding yourself, your true self."

REFLECTIONS: Have you ever obeyed God and discovered your true self in the process? If so, when? What about right now? Are you reserving some areas of your life for yourself? What will it take to make a sacrifice in those areas? What might be the result of doing so?

PRAYER FOCUS: Pray for a willingness to follow Jesus even when it requires sacrifice. Ask Him to show you if you need to make such a sacrifice right now.

42
PASSING JUDGMENT

You, then, why do you judge your brother? Or why do you look
down on your brother? For we will all stand before
God's judgment seat.
ROMANS 14:10

Have you ever been judged by someone? Perhaps someone decided
that you were insensitive or overbearing or arrogant. Without even
knowing exactly how it happened, you were judged and labeled.

Do you remember how unfair it felt? Do you remember the
self-doubt? the frustration?

When we judge another, we subject that person to a similar
uncomfortable, hurtful experience. How does this process unfold?
Well, we examine a person's actions and assign a motive to him or
her. Based on this motive, we assign that person a label: "inconsid-
erate," "uncaring," or even the all-encompassing "jerk." Once we
assign that negative label, we tend to relate to that person based on
it. In a way, the label acts as a negative filter through which we view
that person's behavior. That label becomes that person's identity to
us.

No wonder God so clearly forbids judging others. He wants us
to interact with each other based on a complete picture of each
other, not based on a single, potentially defining characteristic.

I've noticed that when we judge others, we make a series of
erroneous assumptions. First of all, judging another assumes god-
like knowledge. When we judge another, we essentially say, "I
know everything about this person. I know his every motive and
thought. I understand this person completely and am therefore able
to render judgment." We've determined that the person's motives
are wrong and that he or she actively chooses to act errantly. I know

from experience; that's a big assumption.

Second, judging another assumes that the person we label can be defined by a single characteristic. This is one of the most tragic aspects of judging others. Seldom is a person all one thing. A person who tends to complain, for example, might also care deeply for others. Every person is a combination of traits, some positive, some negative. Judgment closes our minds to a person's good traits.

Finally, judging another assumes a right we do not have. When we look down on a brother or sister, we subtly punish that person. Only God has the right to judge and punish. You and I will one day stand together before God's judgment seat. We had best treat each other as fellow servants in the meantime.

Finally, when you're tempted to judge another, just remember how it feels. That memory alone should help you avoid the trap of judgment.

REFLECTIONS: Is there someone in your life right now who you find hard not to judge? What assumptions are you making as you pass judgment on this person?

PRAYER FOCUS: Ask God for the ability to see people through His eyes. Ask for soft hearts, especially as you live and work with each other.

43
A 50-50 PROPOSITION?

*Husbands, love your wives, just as Christ loved the church
and gave himself up for her.*
EPHESIANS 5:25

Admit it: At times you feel put upon by your spouse. Like the time
you felt maneuvered into spending your Saturday morning com-
pleting a "honey do" list instead of playing golf. Or the time he left
an unbelievable mess in the kitchen for you to clean up and never
even thanked you for your efforts. In fact, at times you feel more
than put upon...you feel put out.

The internal monologue goes wild at times like these: *Man, this
just isn't fair. I thought marriage was a 50–50 deal. I'm getting the short
end here!*

A quick reminder, kindly meant: Christian marriage is not a
fifty-fifty deal. In fact, any Christian couple who thinks it is will
undoubtedly have a difficult relationship. Why? If you think marriage should be 50–50, you'll constantly monitor your spouse's
behavior, checking it against your own level of emotional, psychological, and physical investment. *Fine. She helped me last week with
my project. Now it's my turn.* Or the opposite. *Hey, he didn't give me
support last week when I needed it. He'll have to get along by himself
on this one.*

With such an attitude, a growing sense of unfairness will creep
into your relationship and slowly squeeze the life out of it. You'll
start using words like "rights" and "equality." Your marriage will
inevitably metamorphose into a matter of *quid pro quo,* a "fair
exchange." When that happens, you're well on your way to a
marital wasteland. Keeping score just doesn't work in marriage.

Paul's words to the Ephesians quickly shatter the idea of

keeping score in a marriage. "Husbands," he says, "love your wives, just as Christ loved the church and gave himself up for her." Christ sets the example for married love, and His example has nothing to do with fairness. How did Christ love the church? He gave Himself up for her—His blood, His body, His life. In fact, everything He had. He didn't base His loving sacrifice on what we could give Him in return. We do not serve a tit-for-tat Savior.

Marriage, then, if modeled after His love, can't be a 50–50 proposition. No. Its model is crucifixion. Christian marriage requires that each spouse give fully, regardless of return. The standard is "as Christ loved the church," and that means two people giving unconditionally, sacrificing their lives for each other. It means choosing to serve over and over again, even when your own needs aren't always met.

"But it's so hard!" some may say. I agree. The crucifixion of self is no spiritual cakewalk. Neither is it always fair. But our greatest prospect for marital joy centers around our ability to give unconditionally to our partners.

The next time you feel put upon by your spouse, reach inside and find the strength to give with Christ's heart. Get in touch with God's presence and power; ask Him for the strength you need to give freely without keeping score. Then choose to give. Go ahead. You'll be amazed at how God will bless your choice.

REFLECTIONS: Think of one way you can give unconditionally to each other this week. Now share your ideas and affirm your unconditional love.

PRAYER FOCUS: Pray for God's power as you choose to give self-sacrificing love to each other. Ask Him to help you live His kind of love every day.

44

GROWING CLOSE
IN TIMES OF PAIN

I will say of the LORD, "He is my refuge and my fortress,
my God, in whom I trust."

PSALM 91:2

If you've been married for more than a few months, you probably realize that pain sometimes intrudes into your life together. You will, at one time or another, suffer the pain of a financial reversal or a failed friendship or a lost opportunity. As a couple, you'll face crises, transitions, and perhaps even tragedy.

When such times arise, you *can* successfully navigate those rough waters. You must make one decision, however, to guarantee a healthy outcome. It's a simple step, but one that many forget: choosing to pull close to God and to each other in the middle of your difficulties. You must use the opportunity to trust God, incorporating His truth into your lives in a deeper way, while at the same time using the hurricane of pain as an impetus to draw close to each other.

My wife and I discovered the importance of this kind of response some years ago during the greatest tragedy of our lives, the loss of our son. Born two months prematurely, our son David was immediately in trouble. He died six days later. The pain startled us with its intensity, but we didn't face the worst right away. It was two months later, when his due date came and went, and we were left with empty arms and the knowledge that God had allowed it to happen.

That's when the choices began. We continued to face them, not just for a few months but for two years, as we handled our grief. What choices did we make during that time? Though it wasn't easy, Naomi and I decided to talk together about our feelings and to support each other. We chose to pray together, expressing our trust in God and asking for His strength each day. We chose to look deeper into His Word for assurance and help. In short, we pulled close to God and to each other. As a result, our spiritual roots reached deeper as we learned to trust our Lord on a new level. In addition, our relationship grew as we helped each other through the storm.

The winds of adversity may be blowing through your life right now. Perhaps the car has just broken down or one of your children is having trouble in school or your job isn't going so well. How will you respond to God right now? The Psalmist provides a great model: "I will say of the LORD, 'He is my refuge and my fortress, my God, in whom I trust.'" Trust is the salient factor—trust that He loves you, that He's in charge, and that He'll supply what you need. As the Psalmist did, you can choose to trust the Lord.

But in addition, you can choose to move closer to each other by giving support, not blame; dialogue, not distance. Together, pray, plan, and endure. Why not reach out to God together right now, affirming both your trust in Him and your commitment to each other?

REFLECTIONS: Do you face a difficulty that puts pressure on your faith or your relationship with each other? What can you do to successfully weather this storm together?

PRAYER FOCUS: Ask God to help you turn to Him, to trust Him during life's difficulties. Pray for unity so that you can walk through your trials together.

45
YOU MAY NOT HAVE
THE WHOLE STORY

Be completely humble and gentle; be patient,
bearing with one another in love.
EPHESIANS 4:2

Undoubtedly, at one time or another, you've misjudged someone. Perhaps you observed something negative about that person and generalized from there. And you treated this person differently because of your newly formed opinion. You weren't as friendly; you distanced yourself from the relationship. Later you realized that you didn't have the whole picture. By then, it was too late to take back your actions.

I once worked with a pastor who shared the following story with me, a story that reminds me of the importance of treating everyone with respect. Pastor Dave had invited a man to speak at his little country church. Jim came for a week of meetings and stayed with the pastor's family. During the week, Dave invited Jim to do things with him, such as hike in the mountains and visit church members. But every time Dave offered an invitation, Jim said no. Each time, Jim opted to stay in his room.

By the end of the week, Dave was disgusted. He thought the man was lazy, and he had lost a good bit of respect for him. After several days, Dave hardly spoke to him. One thing was certain; he would never invite Jim to speak again.

The week had ended, and Jim was about to drive off when he took Dave aside and spoke to him. "Pastor, I'm sorry to have been so inactive this week. I have cancer, and it makes me very weak sometimes. I wanted to save all my energy for the meetings. I didn't tell you before because I didn't want you to make any extra fuss."

As my colleague finished the story, he said, "Art, you never know if you have the whole story. If I would have been kind to him, my misjudgment wouldn't have damaged our relationship."

We don't always see the whole picture, do we? We observe a scene and put our evaluation on it. We hear something and rush to judgment. But we don't know what a person may have gone through in a day or the challenges he or she faces. We don't know the losses that person may have sustained. If we're quick to judge based on limited information, our relationships will suffer.

Paul provides believers with a wonderful protection against misjudgment. It's simply this: Treat each person with God's love regardless of what you think you know about him or her. "Be completely humble and gentle; be patient, bearing with one another in love."

Humility helps us identify with others. After all, who among us is without fault? *Gentleness* affirms others. If we treat people kindly and gently, regardless of what we think they may have done, we leave room for healing. *Patient love* allows us to continue in relationship with others, giving us a positive entry into their lives. When someone fails, patient love refuses to make global judgments.

See if you can apply this principle to the people in your life today—the waitress who seems a little snippy, the colleague whose work is slipping, the PTA member who always has a different opinion about how things should be done, the church member who seems so cantankerous. Bear with them in humility, gentleness, patience, and love. Leave the judgment to God.

REFLECTIONS: Evaluate yourself. Are you judgmental? Do you tend to evaluate people without seeing the whole picture? How can you put humility, gentleness, patience, and love to work to help you avoid doing this in the future?

PRAYER FOCUS: Pray for God's perspective as you observe the people in your life. Ask Him to help you bear with others in love.

46
EMOTIONAL BONDING
PART ONE: OVERVIEW

Then the LORD God made a woman from the rib he had taken
out of the man, and he brought her to the man.
The man said, "This is now bone of my bones and flesh of my flesh."
GENESIS 2:22–23

I'll admit it; I'm a people watcher. And some of the most interesting people to observe are couples. More than once I've watched older couples walking hand in hand, laughing and talking together. They appear to be touching not only physically but on some deep emotional level. Watching them interact brings to mind couples I've known personally over the years—couples married for twenty, thirty, or even forty years who evidence a deep, satisfying bond of love.

What about you? Do feelings of warmth, excitement, and closeness still emanate between you? If so, why? If not, why not? Maybe it's time to ask yourselves how strong feelings grew between you in the first place and how you can intentionally maintain emotional closeness.

I recently asked a number of couples to describe how they keep feelings alive in their marriages. They mentioned many things including, "Be best friends," "Make your partner feel loved every day," and "Don't let the romance go out of your marriage." They talked about communication, commitment, and prayer.

As I thought about their comments, I began to notice a common thread. Each of these activities helps to establish or maintain an *emotional* bond. There's no one secret action that can ensure a great relationship. The intangible magic I observe in successful couples comes from many different actions, all combining to create a deep emotional bond.

Christian psychologist Henry Cloud says that "bonding is the ability to establish an emotional attachment to another person. It's the ability to relate to another on the deepest level."[1] To bond with each other is to form an emotional attachment between you. You may be thinking, *Hold it. I thought that love is a commitment. You can't just go on emotion.* True, but over the years I've noticed that successful couples, acting out of committed love, do what it takes to deepen the emotional bond between them. Adam's words to Eve, for example, indicate commitment but also express emotional attachment: You are "bone of my bones and flesh of my flesh." Can you feel the warmth and affirmation contained in his words?

The emotional attachment I've discussed doesn't just happen; it takes effort. So what can couples do to generate such bonding? The short answer is this: everything. That's right. Any time a husband and wife interact positively with each other, they generate warmth between them. When these interactions happen again and again in a variety of ways, these shared experiences and feelings of being cared for deepen the relationship. The framework of emotional bonding is built little by little over a long period of time with every positive experience. In the best marriages, this process never ends.

Over the next few days, let's explore specific behaviors that deepen the emotional bond over time. Get set to deepen the warmth, excitement, and closeness you experience as a couple!

REFLECTIONS: Be honest. Do you feel close to each other? Are you emotionally bonding with each other daily?
PRAYER FOCUS: Invite God to help you deepen your emotional bond in the days to come.

47
EMOTIONAL BONDING
PART TWO: CARING

Always try to be kind to each other and to everyone else.
1 THESSALONIANS 5:15

You want to encourage feelings of warmth, excitement, and closeness in your marriage. You want to promote the warm glow of emotional bonding. So how do you do it? One way to build that emotional bond is by reaching out in tangible ways with kind and caring behavior.

When spouses say and do things to please their partners, they demonstrate caring for each other. Such caring may be as simple as a pleasant smile or as elaborate as a thoughtful surprise. A small gift, a warm "thank you," a compliment, or a hug might all indicate caring. Each kind and caring act generates a spark of warmth that forges the emotional bond between a husband and wife.

While you can demonstrate caring in a variety of ways, caring words are a great place to start. To get a quick handle on caring words, think of the "four A's": approval, affection, acceptance, and appreciation. These kinds of words express kindness and caring that will build the emotional bond between you.

Words of *approval* attribute value to each other. When you use them, you recognize each other's strengths and assets as well as each other's efforts to improve. Approving words communicate these messages: "You're a capable person," "You do this very well," "You're really making progress." Frequent compliments are acts of kindness and caring that will encourage your spouse and bring you closer together.

Words of *affection* add the dimension of tenderness and passion to your marriage. Affectionate words communicate these messages: "You're desirable," "I'm drawn to you," "I have deep feelings of love for you." One husband I know occasionally looks at his wife lovingly for a few seconds then says, "I'm just appreciating you; that's all." Those simple words communicate volumes about the deep affection this man feels for his wife.

Words of *acceptance* help you both feel secure. Accepting words communicate these messages: "I'm in your corner no matter what" and "You don't have to win my love with your performance." I was with a couple recently when the wife belittled herself over some weakness. Her husband wisely said, "I'd rather have you as my partner than anyone else." I could almost see the warmth of acceptance flooding this woman's heart.

Words of *appreciation* introduce the aspect of gratitude into your marriage. Think for a moment about how you feel when someone thanks you. It feels great, doesn't it? Appreciative words communicate these messages: "I'm grateful for what you do and who you are," "I'm aware of your great qualities," "I'm thankful for you." Words of appreciation help you feel both wanted and needed.

Of course, you can also express caring with your actions. Giving each other your time and attention speaks volumes. Expressing caring through a loving touch—such as snuggling, hugging, and holding hands—communicates that you care. Doing anything that makes life easier for your spouse is also a kind and caring act that will bring you closer together.

Couples sometimes forget these simple ways of expressing caring. Words and acts of kindness and caring can be forgotten in the hectic schedule of each day. If you want to deepen the emotional bond between you, start thinking, *What can I do each day that will express caring to my partner?*

REFLECTIONS: Think for a moment about the kind and caring behaviors that would increase the "warm fuzzies" between you. Ask each other, "What would you like me to do for you that would demonstrate how much I care?"

PRAYER FOCUS: Ask God to give you sensitivity to each other and an ability to express kindness and caring so you can build up each other.

48
EMOTIONAL BONDING
PART THREE: ROMANCE

Arise, my darling, my beautiful one, and come with me. See!
The winter is past; the rains are over and gone. Flowers appear
on the earth; the season of singing has come, the cooing
of doves is heard in our land.... Arise, come, my darling;
my beautiful one, come with me.
SONG OF SONGS 2:10–13

Has your relationship gone a little flat lately? Same old hello in the morning? Same old schedule during the day? Same old TV shows at night? Same old weekend fare? Same ol', same ol'? Nothing bad happening, but no electricity in the air and certainly no romance?

Emotional bonding is established in many different ways, but romance is definitely near the top of the list. Take a look at Solomon's words to his love in Song of Songs. The excitement, warmth, and emotion of romance permeate every phrase. How do you think Solomon's partner felt as she heard these words? Certainly she must have felt emotionally drawn to Solomon. His warmly and openly communicated wish to be with her most likely produced a tender moment of love and appreciation between them.

If you want to generate some heat, you're going to have to light a fire. That means you may have to replace "same ol', same ol'" with some new behavior. Specifically, you need to find or relearn your partner's love language. That is, discover what makes your spouse feel especially valued, the expressions of love that really mean something to her. That's the key element of romance—making your partner feel deeply valued.

Romance means different things to different people. One husband told me, "Romance is the unexpected little things that Judy does for me. Sometimes she'll make a special coffee and bring it out to me. Sometimes she'll leave a note in my lunch. Romance for me is the unexpected surprise." One wife told me, "My husband won't write a poem for me, but he will use his skill as a carpenter to make special projects that are meaningful to me. That's romantic." Still another wife said, "Romance is feeling truly loved and special. You think, 'He did that just for me.'"

Are flowers romantic? To many women, yes. But what makes them romantic? Simply this: They are a special expression of *value*. Over our twenty-plus years of marriage, I've written my wife several poems. I recently asked her, "Is a poem romantic for you?" Her response was interesting: "I know that you sat down and thought about it. You took your time, chose words, and thought about me. That makes me feel especially loved and important, and because of that, a poem is definitely romantic."

Conversation itself can be romantic. A wife told me recently, "One of the most romantic things my husband can do is talk to me. A meaningful conversation with him definitely makes me feel romantic." Notice the emphasis on *meaningful* conversation. This wife considers meaningful conversations romantic because they communicate value to her. When her husband opens up to her and shares his thoughts, ideas, and emotions, she hears, "I love you. I want to be close to you."

Want to break out of the "same ol', same ol'" rut? Follow Solomon's example. Find your partner's love language and communicate how greatly you value her with your words and actions. The emotional bond between you can't help but deepen.

REFLECTIONS: Tell each other what you find romantic. Think of ways to "speak" in each other's love language. Then do it!
PRAYER FOCUS: Ask God to help you understand each other's love language so you can express how deeply you value each other.

49
EMOTIONAL BONDING
PART FOUR: FRIENDSHIP

Do not forsake your friend…better a neighbor
nearby than a brother far away.
PROVERBS 27:10

Are you each other's best friend? Do you invest more heavily in your couple friendship than in any other relationship? You won't be surprised to know that partners who experience excellent marriages consistently report that they are each other's best friends.

What strikes me about Proverbs 27:10 is the observation that friends do not forsake each other. A friend who is either physically or emotionally "far away" is really not a friend at all. Applied to marriage, it is clear that we need to "be there" for our marriage partners.

The key concept in deepening your couple friendship is expressed in one word: sharing. If you want to develop a deeper friendship and a more intense emotional bond, you must share yourselves and your experiences with each other in a variety of ways.

What do couples share? First, they share *activities and interests.* Couples do things together: activities as mundane as shopping, as exotic as Caribbean cruises, and everything in between. I know a couple who bought a canoe last summer specifically to spend time together and enjoy stimulating conversation and fantastic scenery. They had a great time and created a storehouse of warm memories. Couples can share as they develop hobbies, projects, and leisure activities together. Hiking, biking, cribbage, collecting, gardening, decorating the house, even cleaning the garage—such shared activities foster couple friendship.

Couples who care about their friendship also share their

thoughts and ideas. They talk freely on a variety of levels. They offer opinions that stimulate discussion. They decide to be vulnerable, sharing their ideas, musings, and responses to life's events. When did you last exchange opinions about a political candidate or share how you were applying a certain Scripture in your life? How about that talk you need to have concerning your children? Best friends share what's on their hearts.

Finally, close friends share their *emotions* with each other. Communicating emotions is one of the deepest levels of self-disclosure. Close couples say these words to each other: "I feel...because..." For example, "I feel disappointed because I messed up at work today." Recently I said to Naomi, "With this hay fever going full bore, and all the commitments I'm obligated to in the next several weeks, I'm feeling overwhelmed." Whenever you share these kinds of statements, you let your spouse into your world. As a result, you draw closer to each other.

Maybe you've experienced some distance in your relationship recently. You've become aware that you're not as close as you'd like to be. Simple solution: Learn again to share each other's worlds. You'll experience the intimacy of couple friendship and the closeness of a deepening emotional bond.

REFLECTIONS: Are you deliberately sharing activities, interests, thoughts, ideas, and emotions? Why or why not? What new activities could you pursue that will build your friendship?

PRAYER FOCUS: Pray for a new openness between you. Ask God for guidance as you think of ways to share your world together.

50
MOLEHILLS

*For the grace of God....teaches us to say "No" to ungodliness and
worldly passions, and to live self-controlled, upright and
godly lives in this present age.*
TITUS 2:11-12

Molehills. I hate 'em. A tribe of pesky moles—scores of them—
seem to inhabit various corners of the seven acres on which our
church facility rests. I'll drive onto the property, admire the recently
mowed lawn, then notice a fresh mound of dirt and then another
and another. At these times, I find myself starting to boil. *One of
those moles has been at it again! How dare that critter invade the church
property and leave our lawn cratered with molehills?*

Then something strange happens. I walk into the church office
and promptly forget all about those molehills. I become involved
with other things and simply put the molehills out of my mind. I
drive home that night and scarcely notice them. In the weeks to
come, it crosses my mind that I should do something about the
mole, but then I consider the hassle and just put it off.

Finally, those molehills aggravate me so much that I bring out
the traps. I declare war. "The mole must go!" Sometimes, I actually
catch the wily creature. Relieved, I'm lulled into thinking I've
solved the problem forever. But eventually, that mole's cousins
return for another invasion, and the whole thing starts over again.
The war continues!

What in the world do molehills have to do with living the Christian life? Well, sin bears more than a passing resemblance to
molehills. When you first become aware of a particular sin in your
life, you know it's wrong, and you feel motivated to do something
about it. When you realize that impatience or anger or unforgiveness

habitually intrudes into your life, you don't like what you see. You know that allowing sin to stay in place will leave its mark upon your life, just as those maddening molehills erupt on a pristine lawn.

Then something strange happens. You go about your business, and before you know it, you're ignoring the problem. You become involved in other things and simply put it off. In the back of your mind, you know you should address the issue, but it's so hard. Nobody's perfect, right? And maybe your sin isn't *so* bad. So you decide to forget about it.

But inevitably the problem returns. Pretty soon, those molehills of sin erupt again. You realize after a while that without a direct assault, nothing will change. Naturally, you need the Lord's forgiveness—and, fortunately, He has promised to give it abundantly—but you also need to stand against the sin that intrudes into your life.

Titus 2:11–12 urges believers to pull close to God and tap into His grace. His enabling power and unmerited favor will teach you, Titus says, how to say no to sin. Don't ignore the sin. Don't be overcome by it. Say no to it. Declare war!

REFLECTIONS: Do you have some recurring "molehills" in your life? If you feel safe enough, share these issues with each other.
PRAYER FOCUS: Pray for each other about the areas you find difficult to change. Ask God to forgive you and to help you overcome the sin.

51
ADMIT IT—YOU'RE NEVER GOING TO CATCH UP

Do not wear yourself out to get rich;
have the wisdom to show restraint.

PROVERBS 23:4

Seems like you never get to cross off that last item on your "to do" list these days, doesn't it? There's always something more you should do. If you have children, you're even more likely to find yourselves dragging through the day, wondering if you'll ever catch up.

Bottom line: Families are busy That almost certainly includes yours.

I surveyed some of my friends recently to measure their levels of activity. Maybe you'll relate. Most of my friends have at least three or four children. These children are involved in a plethora of music lessons and sports and church activities. Like human pinballs, these families ricochet from soccer games to school concerts to youth groups, meeting back home in time to start all over again. In addition, they are all heavily involved in church life and ministry positions. They have hobbies, obligations, and interests. And believe it or not, they all find time to earn a living!

Of course, all this activity doesn't even begin to take into account what it means to keep a house running. In their "spare time," parents in these families balance the checkbook and pay the bills. They fix broken appliances, do laundry, and change diapers. They wash dishes continually. They help their children with homework and clean up spilt milk. And it never stops.

Relating yet?

I hate to do this, but now I'm going to remind you of those *additional* tasks that you'd rather forget. What about those dirty curtains that need to be taken down and cleaned? the gutters that need to be emptied of winter's debris? the refrigerator that has mold growing in its deep, inner recesses? the garage that desperately needs to be decontaminated? the lawn that cries out for fertilizer?

What's my point? You can go to bed late and get up early and still not get everything done. And you can go through life with a constantly nagging sense of guilt about what you *aren't* doing and feel driven to get it *all* done. More important, you just might allow the household tasks and the general urge to succeed in everything push you away from maintaining your important priorities: God, marriage, and family.

I have a radical solution. Ready? Here it is: Just admit it—you'll never catch up. There it is, out in the open. Give up on getting *everything* done. You'll always have a task waiting for you somewhere, calling for your attention, and you just won't have time for it. Admit it.

Instead of feeling guilty and pushing ourselves to the limit, why don't we heed the advice of Proverbs 23:4: "Do not wear yourself out to get rich; have the wisdom to show restraint." While this verse addresses how the desire for riches can push us to the breaking point, the principle holds true for all tasks. Here's the Hunt paraphrase for married couples: "Don't wear yourselves out for things that aren't that important; learn to show restraint so that you can live balanced lives."

Relax a little. Lighten up. Make sense?

REFLECTIONS: Do you feel overwhelmed right now? In what areas? What can you do to help each other "show restraint"? Can you think of some task or responsibility that you can release?
PRAYER FOCUS: Pray for wisdom in undertaking your tasks and responsibilities. Ask God to help you find balance in your lives.

52
"I LOVE YOU"

Tell me, you whom I love, where you graze your flock.

SONG OF SONGS 1:7

"I love you." Powerfully important words for every couple in love. The Song of Songs explodes with such passionate declarations. The book sizzles with the language of love, pointing the way for married couples of all ages.

Here's a simple question for you: Do you find ways to speak words of love to each other? Do you say them often and with conviction? Mike Mason speaks eloquently about the importance of such words:

> The words of love are important. It is important that they be heard, and it is important that they be spoken, out loud, no matter how painful this hearing and this speaking might be. It is a marvelous thing when love comes bubbling up like tears in the throat as one is gripped by a sudden stabbing realization of the other's beauty and goodness.... But more imperative still than the speaking of love when it cannot be kept in is the speaking of it when it can, even if the speaking seems almost impossible, even if the words must be choked out.... Perhaps the time to speak will be a time of strife and hurt, or perhaps a time when one or the other's deepest and most incorrigible human weakness shows painfully through, like a splintered bone protruding out of the skin. At such times, like an apology or a confession, an "I love you" can drop thunderous and unexpected and shockingly bright and innocent from the lips.[1]

I suppose I've said "I love you" to my dear wife three or four times a day since we've been married. Twenty-five thousand or so "I love you's" later, I've noticed something. The "speaking of love when it cannot be kept in" as well as the speaking of love when the "most incorrigible human weakness shows painfully through" is becoming more important, not less. The regular assurances of love for each other communicate the continued promise of the marriage relationship. With each "I love you," we declare that nothing can break our bond of married love.

The longer we're married, the deeper our love for each other grows, yet the more we revel in its assurance. Perhaps it's because we have no secrets left between us. We know each other's weaknesses. We see the way in which time takes its toll as we grow older. We're aware of our brittle humanity. Over and over, we want to hear the words "I love you."

Recently, I was with a couple when the husband spontaneously spoke words of love to his wife. Her eyes brightened as she smiled and leaned close to whisper loving words in return. What a graphic reminder of how important those words are and how much every marriage needs them!

Of all the words you say to each other in a typical week, none may be more important than these three: "I love you." Why not find a time and place to say them to each other today?

REFLECTIONS: Evaluation time. Do you say "I love you" to each other regularly? If not, why not? How can you find times and ways to speak these words to each other on a consistent basis?
PRAYER FOCUS: Pray for growth in your ability to express love to each other, especially to say the simple words "I love you."

53
ACTIVE LOVE

Let us not love with words or tongue but with actions and in truth.

1 JOHN 3:18

Wondering how to keep your love for each other strong and growing? This verse contains a simple prescription: Love "with actions and in truth."

Christian psychologist Neil Warren says, "Commitment requires a far more active approach in marriage.... Staying in a marriage can be totally passive; you don't leave, but you don't do anything to make the marriage better."[1] It's possible to be committed to a marriage yet passive about your relationship.

Sometimes we fall into passivity because we think love is a feeling and we wait for it to arise and motivate us. But love is a verb, an action word. Christ modeled such love Himself. He loved the church by giving Himself up for it. Love moved our Lord to action, to sacrifice Himself for our sins. In the same way, a marriage comes alive when a couple decides to *actively* demonstrate their love for each other.

In a growing marriage, there's no room for passivity. Consider the words of your wedding vows, words such as "to love, to honor, to cherish." There's not an ounce of passivity in those promises. Instead, they bring to mind images of loving acts and loving words. Great marriages are ones in which love becomes an activity, something couples *do*.

Think about the couples you know in whom the spark of marital love burns most brightly. When you're around them, watch their actions. As you do, you'll probably observe compliments, caring acts, affirmation, and affection. In other words, you'll see active love, two people who understand how to demonstrate their love in small ways every day. A good marriage doesn't grow into a great marriage unless each person is actively involved in building the relationship.

What do couples do to actively express their love? Surprises, gifts, saying "I love you," back rubs, honest compliments, active sharing, attentive listening, sacrifices, special times away, long walks, holding hands, and loving glances. All of these actions—and a thousand more—demonstrate committed love. Find the language of love that best speaks to each of you, then speak it to each other often.

Perhaps you've been married for a while, and you see no threat to your commitment to each other. Yet more than once, I've counseled couples who have been married for twenty or twenty-five years who, while they don't necessarily fight, have lost all relational electricity. Ironically, the longer you're married, the greater your potential for drifting apart. After all, when you've been married for many years, you can easily slump into an attitude that takes the relationship for granted or slip into a routine and forget that the health of your marriage depends upon active expressions of your love.

Why not do a checkup in your marriage right now? Do small acts of love and kindness happen regularly in your marriage? Do you maintain a constant sense of closeness through these actions? If your relationship isn't all that you want it to be, don't despair! You can make small changes that will make a big difference. For an excellent start, put your love into action.

REFLECTIONS: In what ways do you actively demonstrate your love for each other? Is your relationship growing, or are you slipping into a passive routine that you need to change?
PRAYER FOCUS: Pray for a renewal of your marriage bond and for initiative to actively share your love for each other.

54
WHEN OTHERS FAIL YOU

For Demas...has deserted me.... At my first defense, no one came to
my support, but everyone deserted me. May it not be held against
them. But the Lord stood at my side and gave me strength.
2 TIMOTHY 4:10, 16–17

Have you ever felt deserted? Most believers, at some point in their
lives, face such a challenge. Maybe you're at that point now. You
thought you'd receive support, but you're left high and dry. Someone you thought you could count on has failed you, and you feel
abandoned.

I want to take you to such a point in the apostle Paul's life. In
some of the final words he ever penned, Paul wrote, "For
Demas...has deserted me." This must have been extremely difficult for Paul. Though innocent of any wrongdoing, Paul was
suffering for his faith. He thought he could count on Demas in the
crisis. Now Demas had deserted him.

At this time in his life, Paul evidently underwent an investiga-
tion leading to a trial. He wrote, "At my first defense...everyone
deserted me." You can hear the pain in Paul's words; no one supported him in his time of need. In the particular fight that Paul was
waging, none of the local Christians, none of his longtime associates, stood with him. He must have felt the icy fingers of intense
loneliness.

And then Paul wrote something truly extraordinary: "May it
not be held against them." Paul was no Milquetoast. He wouldn't
have hesitated to condemn acts of evil intent. But he realized that
people are imperfect. They have a tendency to fail. And that means
that even Christians don't always have the strength or patience to
do the right thing, to support a friend in need. Paul realized this.

He must have chosen to see his friends' abandonment as the weaknesses of good people afraid for their lives. Paul didn't waste time and emotional energy on bitter recriminations against those who failed him. He chose to forgive them.

Then Paul revealed his ultimate source of strength during this time: "But the Lord stood at my side and gave me strength." Paul recognized an important fact, one that every Christian needs to remember: Even if everyone else deserts you, the Lord never will. He will stand at your side and give you strength in all circumstances.

By faith, Paul believed the Lord was with him. If you're enduring a crisis, you can bank on this reality too. God will give you the resources you need when you need them. And because this is true, you can refuse to give up. You can choose to persevere. With the Lord standing by your side, you can do anything.

Sometime soon someone will fail you. You'll be tempted to wallow in the mud of bitterness and depression. Instead, know that the Lord stands by your side, and choose to receive the strength He has for you.

REFLECTIONS: How do you tap into God's strength during times of loneliness or abandonment? Do you need to do that right now?
PRAYER FOCUS: In prayer, choose to forgive those who have failed you. Ask God for the ability to sense His presence and receive His strength during such times.

55
ABSOLUTE TRUTH?
ABSOLUTELY!

The Lord was standing by a wall that had been built true to plumb,
with a plumb line in his hand. And the LORD asked me,
"What do you see, Amos?"... Then the LORD said, "Look, I am setting
a plumb line among my people Israel."

AMOS 7:7–8

Are you actively and intentionally involved in your children's moral development? Not long ago I read that a group of Christian teenagers were asked, "Is there such a thing as absolute truth, something that is true in every circumstance?" An alarming percentage of these Christian teens said no. This poll blasts a warning to parents: Take your role as moral teacher seriously.

Daily our children face the clash between God's values and society's relative moral stance. God's "plumb line," His absolute standard of right and wrong, is considered narrow-minded and "intolerant" in our culture. In fact, some of our society's institutions actually work against godly values.

In times like these, we must teach our children God's standards. Our kids need to understand and embrace the difference between God's absolute standards and the worlds' relative ones. Perhaps the following story can help parents explain the essential difference:

Two carpenters decided to build a house. They agreed to work together to build the best house they could. So they gathered their plans and materials and began to build.

The carpenters' first task was to cut a board exactly ten feet long. The first carpenter took off his shoes, stood by the board, and carefully walked ten steps, toe to heel. He then marked the board. As he began to cut it, the second carpenter stopped him.

"That's not right!" the second carpenter exclaimed. "The plans call for a board that is ten feet long."

The first carpenter replied, "I measured ten feet."

"No, you didn't," his partner returned. "You used your own feet to measure. You didn't use a tape measure."

"I don't have to," the first carpenter said. "I can use my own feet as a measure because that's what looks right to me."

What's wrong with this picture? Could the first carpenter build the house successfully, according to plan? Twelve inches, a foot, is a standard of measure that never changes. Any carpenter anywhere can understand and build from blueprints that adhere to this standard. But if a carpenter throws the standard to the wind, who knows what his building will look like in the end?

Just as no one would build a house without standards of measurement, we can't build our lives without God's standards as defined in His Word. Others will try to use their own measurements, but eventually "what looks right to me" will always cause trouble.

What do our children need to know? That God's plumb line never changes. If we live our lives according to His standard, we will build something strong and good and lasting. This truth will do more to help our kids than almost anything else we teach them.

REFLECTIONS: Are you teaching God's absolute standards in your home? How can you actively teach your children that there is such A THING AS RIGHT AND WRONG?

PRAYER FOCUS: Ask God to show you how to teach your children His absolute truth, especially as the world teaches them that truth is relative. Pray for God's protection over them as they navigate through the cultural morass of moral relativism.

56
DON'T WAIT—DO IT NOW

Therefore, as we have opportunity, let us do good to all people,
especially to those who belong to the family of believers.
GALATIANS 6:10

If you're like most people, someone in your circle of friends and family rubs you the wrong way—you know, the person who often says or does something that grates on you. Perhaps the two of you have even experienced conflict. You know God calls you to love that person, but you find it hard to do.

Have that person in mind? Good. Now I want you to try something that will help you with that challenging person. If you can make this action a habit, you will not only learn to work with that person, you will also learn to bless others in your life.

What's the action? When you have an opportunity to do good, don't wait; *do it now.* When you have the tiniest inclination to do or say anything good to someone, don't hesitate. Make it happen now. Why? Because five minutes or an hour from now, you may *not* feel like it, and the opportunity will have vanished.

If you struggle with liking someone, you'll almost always fight negative feelings about him or her. At those times, you'll find it difficult to overcome those feelings enough to do or say something positive. So if you want to change the relationship for the better, *act* on every inclination to do good for that person.

Maybe you're thinking, *Hold it. I thought expressions of love weren't supposed to be based on feelings.* You're right, they're not. Love is a decision. However, one of the best ways to enable yourself to express love when you *don't* feel like it, is to begin expressing love when you *do.*

Several years ago I had almost daily contact with someone with whom I had difficulty relating. It threw me because I generally like people and have an easygoing personality. But in this case, I found myself reacting negatively to this person much of the time. I didn't like what I was feeling and started to look for ways to break out of the negative cycle. That's when I made the decision to do good for this person whenever I could.

My action plan was simple. Whenever I saw this person, I wouldn't wait for him to offend me; I would talk to him. First, I would make sure I gave him a warm greeting (small things count!) with good eye contact and a friendly smile. From that small beginning, I looked for other ways to serve this person. Even choosing to listen to him was a way to do good. The "don't wait—do it now" philosophy made an enormous difference in my attitude and, ultimately, our relationship.

Are you fighting negative feelings toward someone right now? Most of us do from time to time. Why not take advantage of your opportunities today to do good for that difficult person and see what changes God brings in both of your lives?

REFLECTIONS: Is there someone in your life who is difficult to love or to whom it is hard for you to relate? How can you apply Galatians 6:10 to this relationship? How can your partner help you in the process?

PRAYER FOCUS: Pray for the power, ability, and strength to utilize your opportunities for doing good to others, especially those you find difficult to love.

57
PSYCHOLOGICAL AIR

My dear brothers, take note of this:
Everyone should be quick to listen, slow to speak.
JAMES 1:19

Are you "quick to listen"? Many of us aren't, especially in our marriages. Yet it is such an important quality.

Author Stephen Covey aptly describes why listening is so meaningful:

> Empathic listening is...deeply therapeutic and healing because it gives a person "psychological air."
>
> If all the air were suddenly sucked out of the room you're in right now, what would happen to your interest in this book? You wouldn't care about the book; you wouldn't care about anything except getting air. Survival would be your only motivation.
>
> But now that you have air, it doesn't motivate you. This is one of the greatest insights in the field of human motivation: *Satisfied needs do not motivate.* It's only the unsatisfied need that motivates. Next to physical survival, the greatest need of a human being is psychological survival—to be understood, to be affirmed, to be validated, to be appreciated.
>
> When you listen with empathy to another person, you give that person psychological air. And after that vital need is met, you can then focus on influencing or problem solving.[1]

Simply put, *listening* gives you entrance into another's life. Unless you provide the psychological air your marriage partner needs, you probably won't be able to resolve conflict between you, influence your partner positively, or experience the deeper levels of marital intimacy.

A few years ago, I counseled a married couple who provide an excellent example of this principle. Joe and Ellen genuinely loved each other and demonstrated that love in many ways. They did have one problem, however: Joe just didn't know how to listen. He was a decisive person who moved full-steam ahead. Ellen, on the other hand, tended to be quiet and pleasantly compliant. Over time, Joe developed the habit of making decisions without listening to her. He was a steamroller, flattening any objections in his path. He assumed he knew how she felt and what she wanted, but he never really stopped to listen to her. As a result, Ellen slowly wilted in the relationship even though Joe loved her.

As they identified and addressed the issue, learning to listen made all the difference in the world for this couple. I watched Ellen brighten as Joe learned to hear her thoughts, feelings, and ideas. Instead of barreling ahead and getting his way, Joe learned to defer to Ellen based on what he heard from her. Soon they were operating on a new level. She felt validated and affirmed. Joe's decision to listen rejuvenated their marriage and paved the way for deeper intimacy between them.

I don't know about you, but I think most of us are a lot quicker to speak than we are to listen. Rather than make that mistake in your own marriage, why don't you take a moment to think this over together? You'll never regret finding a way to improve the listening habit.

REFLECTIONS: Are you quick to listen to each other? Does each of you feel understood, affirmed, validated, and appreciated by the other?

PRAYER FOCUS: Pray for the skills necessary to be good listeners. More than that, pray for a desire to be "quick to listen," especially to each other.

58
FOR YOU, NAOMI

The LORD is acting as the witness between you and
the wife of your youth,...she is your partner, the
wife of your marriage covenant.

MALACHI 2:14

Here is a simple but powerful truth: When couples marry, they
enter a marriage covenant. God Himself acts as the witness to the
wedding vows exchanged between a man and woman.

This awesome concept was on my mind recently when I wrote
these words to my wife. See if you relate.

This last week, I performed a wedding ceremony. You
know me, Naomi. I love weddings. And this one was
beautiful. The flowers, the music, the words of the ceremony mingled together exquisitely, sending me home
with the warm glow of marital love brightly lit.

The centerpiece of the service was the vows. I love listening to couples speak those wild and weighty promises
to each other. As couples enter into the marriage covenant,
God Himself is a witness to the vows they speak. As we
move toward twenty-five years of married life together,
Naomi, I want you to know how committed I am to the
vows we spoke to each other so long ago.

"I, Art, take thee, Naomi, to be my wedded wife." I
received you as my wife. I receive you still. You are my
partner, and nothing can change that. I loved you enough
to make a lifelong commitment to you. I will continue to
actively pursue our relationship, taking you into my heart
and life.

"To have and to hold from this day forward." You are mine, and I am yours. You are not alone, Naomi, and neither am I. The bond of marital love will deepen our friendship daily. When the storms of life come—and they have come—we will continue to hold onto each other. There is nothing better than to rest in each other's arms.

"For better or worse, for richer or poorer, in sickness and in health." Remember that I signed on knowing that you were not perfect! (Although sometimes I think you are as nearly perfect as a wife could be.) You may think sometimes that you are letting me down or are not measuring up somehow. Not true. But even if you should have one of those "worse" days, or even months, I am for you in whatever circumstances that come. Let them come. The commitment of love I have made to you doesn't depend on sunny days or a certain future.

"To love and to cherish." To enjoy, to prize, to appreciate, to treasure, to respect, to admire, to value—to cherish you is all of these and more.

"Forsaking all others." Of course, I have remained sexually faithful to you. But I have always taken this promise to mean that, after God, my relationship with you will be the most important in my life. You will be my best friend. My deepest affections and most meaningful conversations will be with you.

"So long as we both shall live, according to God's holy ordinance." Please remember that I am with you for the duration. Yes, it's because I love you, because my life would be immeasurably diminished without you. And it is also because God has decreed it. He knows that it is best that we two live the ups and downs of life together, learning to love, to give, and to grow. For all these reasons, I'm here to stay.

"And thereto, I give you my pledge." There it is: a pledge, a covenant. I gave it long ago, but it strengthens with every

passing year. Know that my pledge still holds securely, an anchor in the blasting winds of changing times or passing fancies.

For you, Naomi. A look back that is really a look forward. Who knows how deep our love can flow in the days ahead as we hold true to the vows of our marriage covenant!

REFLECTIONS: Are you remaining faithful to your marriage vows? Do you need to renew them? If so, what areas could most benefit from recommitment to each other? (You may even wish to write each other a letter, reasserting your commitment to your marriage covenant.)

PRAYER FOCUS: Ask God to enable you both to be true to your marriage vows. Ask for renewal in areas that need His touch.

59
GOD'S PURPOSES

For it is God who works in you to will and to act
according to his good purpose.
PHILIPPIANS 2:13

Do you have a sense today that God will use you to accomplish His divine plan and purpose? Do you believe that as He works through you, your efforts will result in something good for you and for others?

This may sound rather grand, but it's God promise to you and to every believer. As you go through your day today, God will work in and through you. Every person you meet, every task you tackle, is potentially a part of His plan.

I don't know about you, but that idea has a tendency to wake me up and make me ask, "What will God do in and through me today?"

Corrie ten Boom recounts an incident from her life that reminds me of how God works in us to accomplish His purposes. After a speaking engagement in Europe, a couple insisted that Corrie come to their apartment. After some hesitation, she finally agreed. At the time, Corrie was elderly and suffered from a heart problem. These issues turned out to be significant because when Corrie arrived at the couple's apartment building, she discovered that their apartment was on the tenth floor and had no elevator accessing it. As she ascended the ten flights of stairs leading to the couple's apartment, Corrie had to sit and rest between each floor. It was a killer climb for someone her age and in her condition.

Corrie candidly admits that she was inwardly complaining the whole way up the stairs. Why in the world did these people have to *insist* that she come to their home? Why was she dumb enough to accept? How painful to have to climb these stairs!

When Corrie finally arrived at the apartment, she met an elderly couple, both in wheelchairs. Wonderfully, she had the opportunity to lead them both to faith in Christ. Somehow, the ten flights of stairs didn't seem so bad when she understood that God had led her up them.

You never know how God will use you to accomplish His purpose.

My friends Dave and Janet were at the SeaTac airport on the way home from a trip together. After gathering their luggage and finding a place to wait for their ride home, they met a man named Brad. It was purely a "chance" meeting. As the three of them became acquainted, Brad told Dave and Janet that he was new to the Seattle area. As they talked, Dave and Janet discovered that Brad had bought a house south of Seattle that was located about five minutes from their house. Janet invited Brad to church, and he came the following weekend. He and his family have attended Dave and Janet's church ever since.

I wonder how many such divine appointments we miss because we're not attuned to God's purpose and ready for Him to use us.

As a new day begins, be alert for opportunities God presents to you. The note God wants you to write, the word of encouragement to someone, the kindness to your fellow worker, could be a tangible reflection of God's will operating in your life. As you respond, God will accomplish His purpose in and through you.

And if God asks you to climb some stairs, do it!

REFLECTIONS: Share a time with each other when you felt God was prompting you to do something to serve or help another. How did that situation turn out?

PRAYER FOCUS: Ask God to give you sensitivity to His leading and a willingness to act according to His good purpose.

60
KEEP SWINGING!

Never give in then, my dear brothers, never admit defeat; keep on working at the Lord's work always, knowing that, in the Lord, you cannot be laboring in vain.

1 CORINTHIANS 15:58 (NEB)

Babe Ruth was one of the most phenomenally gifted players in the history of baseball, hitting 714 home runs in regular-season play. His lifetime batting average, achieved in 2,500 games over a twenty-two year career, was .342. This man was one of the premier baseball players of all time.

What, you ask, could Babe Ruth possibly have to do with 1 Corinthians? How about this: During his baseball career, Babe Ruth struck out 1,330 times. I can draw only one conclusion from this fact: We need to keep swinging! Paul said it this way: "Never give in...never admit defeat." In other words, no matter how many times you've struck out, grab that bat again and keep swinging!

Paul exhorts us to persevere in the "Lord's work," but what does that term mean? I think it can mean a variety of things. It might include an internal enterprise—something you're working on in your own character, such as patience or a forgiving heart. It might also include your ministry focus. Or the Lord's work might mean building a Christ-honoring relationship with another person.

Let me ask you this. Have you considered your marriage as the Lord's work? I can assure you that your marriage relationship is exactly that. Think of all that it takes to establish and maintain a healthy relationship. Consider the attitudes you need to foster, the skills you need to develop, and the many acts of love and kindness you perform each day. If that's not the Lord's work, I don't know what is.

In most marriages, ongoing issues arise from time to time. Perhaps one of you tends to withdraw when angry. Or maybe one of you consistently makes commitments without consulting the other. These issues surface and resurface throughout your married life. They require frequent attention.

And that's the problem. As we continue to address issues again and again, whether in our marriages or in other aspects of the Lord's work, we sometimes become discouraged. Our actions don't always match our intentions, or we don't see the results we'd like to see.

Admit it. You sometimes want to quit. You wonder if your efforts can really change things for the better.

At such times, you need a healthy dose of Babe Ruth and 1 Corinthians 15:58 to encourage you to keep swinging. Sure, you'll strike out sometimes. For every victory, there are some defeats. But you don't have the luxury of quitting. "Never admit defeat," Paul says. Don't give up on the work God wants to do in and through you.

Have you struck out your last six times at bat? Are you tempted to give up, give in, or cop out? I'll tell you something. Unless you keep swinging, you have precisely zero chance of moving forward. Through setbacks, discouragement, or pain, keep doing what's required to accomplish God's work. And if you ever feel like giving up, remind yourself that a home run might be just around the corner.

REFLECTIONS: Have you recently been tempted to give up on some aspect of the Lord's work? If so, talk to your partner about it.
PRAYER FOCUS: Ask God to give you endurance whenever you face failure or discouragement while doing His work.

61
A LITTLE HARD WORK

All hard work brings a profit,
but mere talk leads only to poverty.
PROVERBS 14:23

Have you recently discussed something you'd like to see in your life or family or marriage? Maybe you've talked about it for months or even years but have found it difficult to exert effort toward making the change. At times like these, it's easy to put such an idea back on the shelf to collect dust until the next dream session takes place.

Ted Engstrom, author and president emeritus of World Vision, has some apt words for those of us facing this situation:

> The real winners in life work hard for what they get. But what about the great people who've blessed us with their art, science, and invention? Did their genius come easily? Let's listen to some of them. Thomas Edison said, "Genius is one percent inspiration, ninety-nine percent perspiration." Michelangelo said, "If people knew how hard I worked to attain my mastery, it wouldn't seem so wonderful after all." Carlyle, British man of letters, wrote, "Genius is the capacity for taking infinite pains." Paderewski said, "A genius? Perhaps. But before I was a genius, I was a drudge."[1]

Engstrom makes a simple-but-eloquent point: Nothing worthwhile comes easily. Life most often rewards those who are willing to roll up their sleeves and get busy. Mere talk doesn't get us anywhere.

The book of Proverbs backs up Engstrom's words: "All hard work brings a profit." It's true that hard work applied to a business will probably result in monetary profit, but this principle works in most other areas too. Hard work in your marriage will bring a closer relationship with each other. Hard work in your family life will mean stronger family ties. You can even apply this principle to your spiritual lives.

Nothing worthwhile comes easily. Nothing.

My Uncle Brooks took up golf at the age of forty. Within one year, he was a par golfer. I asked him how he conquered the notoriously difficult game. In his slow Texas drawl, he told me. "Nothing to it, Art. I took lessons every week and played golf every day for a year. It's a wonder what hard work will do for you." He attributed his skill to one thing: hard work. If someone can make that kind of commitment to golf and improve so radically, imagine what would happen if you committed yourself to something of spiritual or relational value!

A couple I knew years ago concluded that they were growing apart and needed to work on their relationship. They decided that on every Saturday morning they'd take a long walk together and use the time for conversation. When they returned, they'd pray together for just a few minutes. They made a commitment. They put energy and time into something they thought was worthwhile. As a result, they experienced a far greater sense of oneness in their relationship. Their hard work brought a profit.

What area of your life needs a little work? Your marriage? Your spiritual life? Your family? What can you commit yourself to that will make a real difference in your life? Whatever it is, take that step today. You'll be amazed at what a little hard work will do.

REFLECTIONS: What have you been putting off that you know would be good for you as an individual or as a couple? Discuss it with each other.

PRAYER FOCUS: Ask God for strength and resolve to invest your energy in what really matters.

62
GOD'S TIMING IS ALWAYS RIGHT

*"Lord," Martha said to Jesus, "if you had been here, my brother
would not have died. But I know that even now God will give
you whatever you ask." Jesus said to her, "Your brother will
rise again." Martha answered, "I know he will rise again
in the resurrection at the last day." Jesus said to her,
"I am the resurrection and the life."*

JOHN 11:21–25

I'm positive that as a couple you've felt the vice-grip of stress.
Probably no emotion is more common to all of us than the pressure
we feel when things don't work out as we'd like. You may struggle
with a difficult situation at work, an illness, or some other crisis.
You feel stuck in the middle with no end in sight. *Where is God?*
you wonder. *What is He doing?* The stress mounts. *Surely,* you
think, *now is the time for God to act.*

I suppose no narrative illustrates this sense of tension better
than Lazarus' story in John 11. Mary, Martha, and their brother
Lazarus were close friends of Jesus. When Lazarus became gravely
ill, Mary and Martha naturally turned to Jesus. They sent Him a
note explaining that Lazarus was sick. "Come quickly," they
implored.

Can you picture Mary and Martha waiting for Jesus' arrival,
watching the road, listening for the sound of His approach? Can
you imagine their stress mounting? "Where *is* He? Doesn't He
know how important this is?"

Finally, in what must have been a heart-rending moment for
this family, Lazarus died. Jesus' friend was "alone" in his final
moments. Christ had not appeared.

Four days later, however, Jesus did arrive. Mary and Martha, filled with grief, told Him of their pain. "If you had been here," they said. "If only…" You can hear the crushed hope in their voices, the faint glimmer of what might have been.

You know the rest of the story. Just minutes later, Jesus raised Lazarus from the dead in a glorious display of God's power and love.

My question: Was Jesus on time or not? My answer: yes and no. He wasn't fast enough for Mary and Martha, but He was *exactly* on time to fulfill God's good purpose for the situation. What appeared to be a mistake was actually part of His ultimate will.

Is stress mounting quickly for you as you negotiate a difficult situation? Do you long for God to act decisively to solve a problem in your life, yet see no solution in sight?

At times like this, remember: God's timing is always right. We can't answer all the why questions. There are no pat solutions for those who pace the floor over some medical, financial, or personal difficulty. But I do know one thing: We can trust that God's timing is right. We can rest instead of pace. We can allow His presence to displace the anxiety that grips the heart.

Believe me, the One who is the "resurrection and the life" has you in mind at this very moment. Whatever your situation, why not join hands right now and affirm your trust in Him?

REFLECTIONS: What stressful situation do you face? Can you see God's timing at work?

PRAYER FOCUS: Take your current situation to God, expressing your need and trust. Then rest in Him for a moment, drinking in His presence and love.

63
BALANCING ACT

Do not love the world or anything in the world. If anyone loves
the world, the love of the Father is not in him.

1 JOHN 2:15

As my family finished watching the movie, I knew I had made a
mistake. I looked at the kids sprawled around the family room. We
thought we'd have fun watching a movie together. Our selection
was rated PG. I assumed it would be acceptable for the family to
watch. It turned out that the bad language so pervasive in films
today permeated this particular video.

"Guys," I told my family, "forgive me for not pulling the plug
on this movie after the first scene. I kept thinking it would get better. I'll do my best not to allow that language in our home again."

It's a balancing act these days, isn't it, being *in* the world but not
of it? I imagine your family has felt the pressure of maintaining that
balance, too. The pervasive influence of movies, theater, television,
and the internet seems to have America in a moral vice-grip,
squeezing us, attempting to break down biblical values.

So how do we do it? The "world" referred to in 1 John 2:15—
the human systems of thought and values as expressed in
society—is such a strong influence. How does God expect us to
maintain our citizenship in heaven while living in a world stained
by sin?

First, I suppose, we should know that God understands the
balancing act we face. He recognizes that we live on a sinful planet;
He Himself lived here on foreign soil and felt the same pressures
we do. And our Father intends that we operate within this society;
after all, He *has* placed us here, and we can't influence others for
Christ unless we operate within the world.

But God also knows that this isn't easy for us, that we need some help. His Word gives us the key to maintaining the balance: "Do not love the world." John isn't talking about shunning the physical environment of this earth (it's all right to be a nature lover!). Nor is he saying that we should deny ourselves the simple pleasures of life, such as a piece of pecan pie or a good mystery novel. What John *does* say is simply this: Do not let your affinity for the things of this world influence you to embrace human systems of thought and action that are antagonistic to God.

The balancing act is clear: Live in the world, but do not love the world. Keep your deepest affections reserved for your heavenly Father. When you rent a movie or cruise the internet or even listen to the evening news, say no to any entertainment that you know is displeasing to God.

You may feel the world's influence pressing in on you and your family even now. Why not take a step back and discuss how you can successfully perform the balancing act?

REFLECTIONS: Have you let entertainment or other activities move your family away from God? Do you exercise spiritual discernment and say no to those things that would compromise biblical values? If not, what's one change you could make that would help restore a better balance?

PRAYER FOCUS: Ask God to give you insight about entertainment or other activities that may compromise your relationship with Him. Ask the Lord for help in guarding your family against the wrong influences of the world.

64
FAMILY VALUES

When I was a boy in my father's house, still tender, and an only child
of my mother, he taught me and said, "Lay hold of my words with
all your heart; keep my commands and you will live."

PROVERBS 4:3–4

Over the last few years, it seems that many politicians have adopted
family values as their pet issue. Yet for all the talk, the Ten Commandments may no longer be exhibited and promoted in
America's schoolrooms. God's most basic value statements have
been rejected in our nation's schools. Sadly, a secular society is
emerging from this country's Christian roots.

While we may be saddened by this trend, we need not be dis-
heartened. Throughout history, Christians have lived and thrived
in societies in which moral deterioration has gutted the heart of the
populace. Somehow, those Christians learned to live out their love
for God and teach their children to do the same. If you have little
ones, I know you're vitally interested in helping them grow up to
understand and practice God's values. And you *can* succeed.

One of the most important things parents can do to instill
godly values in their children is demonstrated in Proverbs 4:3–4. In
this passage, Solomon recalls times during his boyhood when his
father, King David, explained right and wrong to him. A key
phrase is tucked away in this description. Solomon explains that his
father taught him while he was "still tender." A moral foundation
must be poured early in life to be most effective. A tender heart will
receive the biblical values of a loving parent.

Your children's tender years are ripe with teachable moments.
During the normal course of family life, you can communicate

God's values to your young ones. As you take advantage of those moments and intentionally create others, you'll lay a foundation of moral teaching that will impact your children's hearts forever.

I remember a bedtime discussion I had not too long ago with my youngest daughter. Sarah asked me why I was attending the school board meeting that night. In words that my ten year old could understand, I told her I wanted to make sure our schools don't promote ideas that are against God's Word. (In my opinion, the school policy was promoting homosexuality.) This led to a discussion of God's standards for marriage: one man for one woman for life.

Though the school board may want to say differently, I told Sarah, God's standard for marriage is for one man to marry one woman and make a family with her for life. That night, Sarah heard God's family values. Before I tucked her in, we prayed together that the school board would understand what was right and wrong.

I know the task looks big. As a parent, you're working against powerful forces. Truth is up for grabs, it seems. You've probably wondered how in the world you can counteract the lies of a secular society. But believe me, with God's help, you can do it. As you teach and live biblical values, you'll build a moral foundation in your children's hearts that will last a lifetime.

REFLECTIONS: What values do you want to communicate to your children? Together, brainstorm a list of values and ways to teach them. Then pick a value to emphasize over the next few weeks.
PRAYER FOCUS: Ask God to protect your children's minds and hearts from relative "truth." Ask God for guidance as you teach your children in formal and informal ways.

65
SOARING

I will never forget your precepts,
for by them you have preserved my life.
PSALM 119:93

Since the first day of our vacation in Mexico, I had considered it. Naomi had become increasingly nervous as I voiced my intentions. But I couldn't help it—it looked like so much fun! Finally, the opportunity arose as we walked along the crowded beach one afternoon.

I talked to the handsome Mexican in charge. Soon I was convinced and Naomi was resigned. "Go ahead," she said, smiling. "Just don't get hurt."

"Okay," I said to my new Mexican friend, "I'm ready to go." He grinned and began to explain what I had to do. *Wow!* I thought. *It's going to happen. I'm going to be airborne via a three-hundred-foot cable and a powerful speedboat.* Parasailing! I could hardly wait.

"Hold it," I said, "I just thought of one more question: Do people ever get hurt doing this?"

"You bet," he said without hesitation. I gulped. He didn't seem that concerned about it. I decided to probe a bit.

"Why do they get hurt?" I asked.

"They get hurt because they don't do what I tell them."

Suddenly he had my attention. Something inside me became very still, and I decided to give this man my total concentration. He continued for a moment, telling me the basics.

As he finished his instructions, he said, "Now remember, when you see my men wave that red flag, pull hard on the right cord. Got it?"

I nodded. Since he had given those instructions not less than five times during our conversation, I definitely "got it."

In a moment's time, I was 300 feet above the Mazatlan beach.

For the next ten minutes, I soared. The wind held me in its cocoon and carried me along. Nothing below me but the wide, wonderful ocean. It was magical. My childhood dreams of flying had come true!

Any guesses as to what happened when I saw the men on shore waving that red flag? Right! I pulled down hard on the right cord and returned safely to shore. It's amazing how well you listen to instructions when your safety depends on understanding and obeying what you hear.

The writer of Psalm 119 would agree, I think. Essentially he says, "I won't forget what's contained in your Word because, after all, my spiritual life depends on it. That's how I've avoided spiritual mistakes that would have taken me in the wrong direction and threatened my spiritual life."

The Psalmist understood the importance of taking God's Word seriously. He knew it was his guide, that following it would take him soaring to the heights that God had planned for him and would take him safely where he needed to go. That was all the motivation he needed.

God surely wants His children to soar in life, to attain the heights He has planned for them. Unless we listen to His Word and understand His boundaries, however, life will be a mighty dangerous flight. When I saw the potential dangers in my parasailing adventure, I made sure I listened closely to my instructor. In the same way, those who want to soar in life's adventure need to listen to God.

Have you been finding your flight bumpy lately? Have you recently endured some hard landings? Take a tip from God's Word: "I will never forget your precepts, for by them you have preserved my life."

REFLECTIONS: Have you been reading God's Word regularly? Have you recently heard Him say "Now remember..." to you? Which of God's precepts will help you soar?

PRAYER FOCUS: Pray for fresh motivation to read and obey God's Word.

66
MONEY MATTERS
PART ONE

*"Again, it will be like a man going on a journey, who
called his servants and entrusted his property to them.
To one he gave five talents of money, to another two talents, and
to another one talent, each according to his ability.
Then he went on his journey.... After a long time the master of
those servants returned and settled accounts with them."*
MATTHEW 25:14–15, 19

Do you ever find tension about finances nosing its way into your
relationship like an unwanted guest? It's a common marital problem. In fact, money has the potential of causing more trouble
between husbands and wives than virtually anything else. Whether
a couple has a little or a lot, conflict can erupt as spouses struggle to
manage their money.

I imagine that you'd like to reduce that tension in your marriage. Let me give you a suggestion: Gain a common
understanding of what God expects in the area of finances. When
you both agree on a set of core principles, a lot of confusion, not to
mention conflict, clears up. Your question changes from "How do
we get what we want?" to "How can we honor God in our
finances?" Quite a change.

The parable of the talents in Matthew 25 provides couples with
three key principles basic to a biblical understanding of money.

First, you need to understand that *God owns everything.* As
simple as this sounds, it is *the* key to a healthy view of money.
Notice that in the parable, the master went away and "entrusted *his*
property" to his servants. Every resource we have belongs to God,
including our money.

And with ownership comes the right to control. If you view

the money that comes into your family as belonging to you, then you'll spend it however you choose. That attitude is a prescription for money troubles. But when you recognize that your money truly belongs to God, you begin to seek His priorities for investing it as He desires.

Which brings us to the second key principle: *You are managers of what God owns.* Every dollar that comes into your possession belongs to God; however, He has entrusted its management to *you.* The master in Matthew 25 entrusted his wealth to his servants, expecting them to use it wisely and to reap a return. In the same way, God wants you to responsibly use what He has given you for blessing your family and others. Someday you'll stand before your Master; He'll want to know if you did the best you could with what He gave you.

Finally, to manage well what God has given you, *you need to understand His priorities* and make decisions that will honor those priorities. If you're like me, you can easily get caught up in the temporary gratification of things and forget about what God deems most important. It's wise then to sit down together occasionally and ask, "Are we managing the money God gives us in accordance with His priorities? Are we giving, saving, and consuming in proper balance?"

Do you want to ease the tension you may be feeling over money? Start by seeking together to understand God's expectations regarding your finances.

REFLECTIONS: Do you feel that God is in control of your finances? Are you managing the resources He has given you in a wise and balanced way? Do you need to make any changes?

PRAYER FOCUS: Thank God for the financial resources He has placed in your care. Ask God to help you submit to Him and to manage money with His priorities in mind.

67
MONEY MATTERS
PART TWO

*Honor the LORD with your wealth, with the firstfruits of all
your crops; then your barns will be filled to overflowing,
and your vats will brim over with new wine.*
PROVERBS 3:9–10

Would you like financial freedom as a couple? "Dumb question,"
you might say. "Of course we would!" Have you considered the
fact that honoring God with your wealth is the best way to achieve
financial freedom? The reason is simple. When you honor God
with your money, you make financial choices consistent with His
Word. Choosing to manage your finances in light of biblical principles can't help but bring greater financial freedom.

The question, then, is this: What practical decisions can you
make that will honor God with your wealth? I have four suggestions:

First decision: Eliminate your credit cards. While Scripture doesn't
absolutely forbid credit, it certainly makes a case against it.
Proverbs 22:7 says, "...the borrower is servant to the lender." Such
financial slavery does nothing but add pressure to married life.
Eliminating credit may be the best decision you can make to help
prevent financial conflicts and bring honor to God.

What's the alternative to buying on credit? Saving for items
you need, then paying cash. Naturally, this will be hard sometimes
and may mean that you have to wait for things you need or want.
But this system will save you from the crushing burden that consumer debt places on a marriage. It will also teach you to trust God
in a greater way as you watch Him provide for you.

Second decision: Establish a budget. A budget will help you avoid
the trap of consumer debt and the pressure debt brings. It will elimi-

nate guesswork. In order to develop such a spending plan, you will have to sit down and talk about how you both want to spend your income. Resources abound for helping couples make a budget. Larry Burkett's books on the subject are among the best. If you don't have a budget, Burkett's books will offer practical advice.

Third decision: Establish a tithe. Proverbs 3:9 says to bring the "firstfruits of all your crops" to God. This verse describes a tithe, in which we designate a percentage of our income—usually 10 percent or more— specifically for Christian ministry. The tithe is an essential practice for managing money in a way that honors God. When we were first married, my wife and I decided to tithe, and I can honestly say that God has never failed to care for us financially. God has honored our decision to tithe, blessing us financially year after year.

Fourth decision: Pray together about your finances. When couples take their financial concerns to God, they join together in unity. The pressures tend to ebb as they commit their needs to the Lord and submit to His will. Couples who pray together find that God meets their needs in unique ways. Instead of worrying together, pray together!

Do you feel that your finances are out of control? Whether you're teetering on the brink of financial disaster or simply facing the daily pressure of managing your money, these four decisions will help bring order to the chaos. Honoring God with your wealth will make all the difference.

REFLECTIONS: Do you handle money in a way that honors God? Would any of the four decisions described above make a difference? How could you implement positive changes?

PRAYER FOCUS: Pray for unity and wisdom as you evaluate your finances together and make changes in your habits. Ask God to help you honor Him in this area of your marriage.

68
MONEY MATTERS
PART THREE

*"Which of you, if his son asks for bread, will give him a stone?... If you,
then,... know how to give good gifts to your children, how much more
will your Father in heaven give good gifts to those who ask him!"*
MATTHEW 7:9, 11

The year 1975 saw two important firsts in my life. That summer I
was married, and the following fall I snagged my first post-college
job as a high-school English teacher. I made a whopping $8,900 a
year. After taxes that worked out to about $600 a month. Since
Naomi was finishing college and we had to pay for her schooling
each quarter, we didn't have much room for error in our budget.
Our $600 had to stretch a long way.

At the end of my first year of teaching, I was required to attend
summer school to complete my standard teaching certificate.
Naomi still had a year left at the University of Washington. As we
looked at our finances, it seemed clear that our income could not
pay for both her tuition and mine that summer. What would we
do? We literally did not have enough money to do what we needed
to do.

We knew God would have to provide, but frankly, as a newly
married couple, we were concerned. We knew God was capable
and that we could trust Him, but we just couldn't see how He
would provide for this need. One day we were reading Scripture
together and came across a passage encouraging us to pray for our
needs then trust Him to provide. We decided that Naomi's tuition
was something God wanted to provide for us. As we asked Him
for His provision, we both felt that trusting Him meant thanking
Him even before we received it. Every day as we prayed together,
we gave glory to God: "Thank you, Father, for caring about us.

Thank you for providing this tuition money for us."

As the summer approached, we saw no unexpected checks in the mail. What was God doing? How would He provide?

We soon found out. One day as I ate lunch in the faculty lounge, I received a phone call. I couldn't imagine who would call me at school. Was there an emergency? No, it was Naomi with news that just couldn't wait. Her story poured out in short order. Without her knowledge, her professors at the University of Washington had submitted her name for a scholarship. At a department luncheon that day, they had awarded her a full-year scholarship for her final year of college. God had met our need!

God hasn't always met our needs so dramatically, but I will tell you this: He has *always* provided. Our decision to pray together about our finances has been such a relief valve over the years. We've taken our needs to God and have discovered again and again that our Father knows how to give good gifts to those who ask Him.

Do you have a need today? Whatever it is, join together in prayer and ask God to supply. Your Father in heaven has good gifts in store for you.

PRAYER FOCUS: No discussion today. Simply commit your finances to God. Thank Him for His constant provision. And agree together in prayer for whatever you need.

69
A LESSON IN ASKING

Only Luke is with me. Get Mark and bring him with you, because he is helpful to me in my ministry.... When you come, bring the cloak that I left with Carpus at Troas, and my scrolls, especially the parchments.
2 TIMOTHY 4:11, 13

Do you find it difficult to ask each other for what you want or need? Many couples do. I've observed, however, that when marriage partners don't make direct requests, they tend to communicate indirectly about whatever needs they have. Worse, a husband or wife may lock a need inside for a long time, then erupt in anger when that need goes unmet. I think you'd agree that neither option is good.

Examine Paul's words to his close associates, and you'll see that Paul reaches out for help and requests what he needs. He doesn't have too much pride to let his friends know how they can help him personally and in his ministry. Neither does he have any false notions about Christians not having needs.

I remember an instance when our daughter Sarah, who was five years old at the time, walked into our bedroom at 5:30 A.M. What did she want? What emergency couldn't wait until one hour later, when we would be up anyway? What was so earthshaking that she couldn't put it on hold?

I heard her soft voice from Naomi's side of the bed...a sweet, five-year-old voice. "Mommy, I need a hug and kiss." Naomi smiled and wrapped her arms around our daughter and kissed her. Sarah settled into Naomi's embrace for a moment, leaning against the side of the bed, then straightened up and said, "I love you, Mommy," and marched back to her room. I'm sure she was asleep instantly!

Children teach us so much. No pride. No introspection. Just, "I have a need. Will you meet it, please?" That early morning beside our bed, Sarah reminded me that we need to allow ourselves to be needy, to admit our needs, and to ask someone to meet them. That's our best chance of having our needs met.

Think about it. Can your spouse read your mind? Not likely. Once, in a counseling session, a young wife said to me, "If he loved me, he'd figure out what I need." Not necessarily. We husbands can be extraordinarily dense sometimes. Your partner will not know what you want and need unless you communicate those needs. It's just that simple.

Some people—and you may be one of them—find it very difficult to actually say what they want. Maybe you feel selfish when you share a need, or you find it embarrassing to admit that you're needy. Follow Paul's example: Admit your need, and make a direct request. Here's a simple format for communicating your needs: "I need/would like...because..." In practice, it might sound something like this: "I'd appreciate it if you could take Mike to his soccer practice this Saturday, because I have a project I need to complete that morning." Or this: "It would mean a lot to me if we could plan a weekend away. I feel we need to catch up with each other."

Go ahead! Ask already!

REFLECTIONS: Do you feel comfortable making requests of each other? Why or why not? How well do you respond to each other when one of you makes a request? How can you encourage each other to ask directly when you have a need?

PRAYER FOCUS: Ask God for the ability to ask each other for what you want or need. Pray for responsive hearts to meet each other's needs, too.

70
THE SECRET OF
BEING INTERESTING

The purposes of a man's heart are deep waters,
but a man of understanding draws them out.

PROVERBS 20:5

If you're like me, you want others to find you interesting. You want to make new friends and have something to offer those around you. You want to be the kind of person people can talk to so they feel understood and supported. And you want this especially in your relationship with your spouse.

How can you be this kind of person? Listen to the advice of Christian psychologist Alan Loy McGinnis:

> There is a simple secret that will make you interesting. You simply must know how to listen. I still remember the day I went to Bill Carruth, who had come to our little Texas town to teach. He was the sharpest dresser, the wittiest and most urbane man I'd ever met, and for some reason he had taken an interest in a quiet and awkward boy.
>
> "Mr. Carruth," I said, "I wish you could teach me how to talk with people the way you do. I can never think of anything to say."
>
> "Loy," he replied with a wink, "the secret of being interesting is to be interested."
>
> That simple advice has worked for me in 25 years of dealing with people, largely in public life, where I have had to meet and know thousands of individuals. Ask questions the other person will enjoy answering. Encourage people to talk about themselves.[1]

The simple fact is that people want to be known, and no one wants to be known by you more than your marriage partner. People—

including your spouse—are afraid of revealing who they are, but they also long for someone to listen to and really hear them. When you take time to listen, almost inevitably people will reveal their true nature and appreciate you as a kind, caring, and interesting person for doing so.

Proverbs 20:5 makes an astute observation: "The purposes of a man's heart are deep waters." In other words, people are complicated. They don't easily share what's in their hearts. But listen to the rest of the verse: "A man of understanding draws them out." The word picture here is so graphic. Picture someone lowering a bucket into a well then drawing up water. As McGinnis illustrates, if you want to draw from the deep waters of another's heart, you'll have to learn to listen. Ironically, if you say less and listen more, people will find you more interesting.

I must confess that I'm naturally an extrovert. My inclination is to talk, not listen. Yet over the years I've found that people do not respond nearly as well to me when I talk as when I listen. Any bore can ramble on about himself or his ideas. It takes a man or woman of wisdom to draw out others.

This certainly holds true for the marriage relationship. If you show interest in your spouse, asking him questions that will draw him out and giving good eye contact as he speaks, you'll be amazed at the "deep water" you'll draw out.

Try it this week. In your conversations, ask questions that others— especially your spouse—will enjoy answering. Keep encouraging them to talk about themselves. Pay attention to what they say, and occasionally paraphrase what you hear. At work, at home, at church, and especially in your marriage, draw out the deep waters of others' hearts with a listening ear. You'll be amazed at what you discover about those around you...especially about the one you love.

REFLECTIONS: Do you tend to talk more than listen? How can you show interest in others, especially in your mate?
PRAYER FOCUS: Ask God to give you a genuine interest in and love for people as well as a growing ability to listen to their hearts.

71
GOD'S STRENGTH
IN THE STORM

I can do everything through him who gives me strength.
PHILIPPIANS 4:13

I walk into John and Becky's house, hugging my friends and telling them how sorry I am to hear the news. They're grieving over the tragic loss of Becky's brother, Michael, earlier that week. When his car ran out of gas one dark November evening, he decided to walk to a pay phone. On his way back, a passing vehicle accidentally struck him, killing him instantly.

As I talk to this couple, Becky tells me about her brother. She shares some good and some bad. "He was a believer, though," she says. "I know he's with the Lord."

We talk, and there are some tears. But along with those tears I see hope and peace reflected in John's and Becky's eyes. I've seen such peace before in the eyes of believers. I recognize it as God's gracious hand providing what they need. Becky smiles, "I know that God will give us the strength we need to go through this." I nod and smile because I know it too.

As we talk, I remember a familiar passage of Scripture, "I can do everything through him who gives me strength." Sometimes I've been tempted to doubt the "everything" in this verse. Everything, God? Even weathering the death of a loved one or enduring the other losses that intrude into our lives?

But the passage leaves no loopholes. He will help us through *everything*. His strength will flow to us in union with Christ as He infuses our hearts with His presence and His adequacy. *How* it happens, I don't know. *That* it happens—this I know.

You've felt God's hand providing strength in a time of need, haven't you? And along with it, you've received His hope and faith.

Even in tragedy, you've felt your Father's arms around you, holding you in the midst of a storm, comforting you until you could go on. It's supernatural, this blessing of God's strength in the midst of trials.

We pray together, John, Becky, and I. As we do, I ask for God's peace and strength to sustain them. We feel the whisper of God's presence as we pray. We linger for a moment. We know He'll do what He has promised.

As I walk out the door, I feel sad for my friends but renewed in my spirit. I've seen God provide for His children again. I know that when I need His strength and power, it will be there. I smile and breathe in the autumn air. I can do everything through Him who gives me strength.

REFLECTIONS: When have you especially needed God's strength? As you look back on that crisis, loss, or challenge, describe how God helped you.

PRAYER FOCUS: Pray that God will deepen your walk with Him so that when crisis comes, you'll be able to tap into His strength and power.

72
OUR ENTERTAINMENT

*Since, then, you have been raised with Christ, set your hearts on
things above, where Christ is seated at the right hand of God.
Set your minds on things above, not on earthly things.*

COLOSSIANS 3:1–2

Do you ever feel that your family's entertainment choices fall a bit
short of Colossians 3:1–2? I do. Videos and cable television offer a
mind-boggling assortment of entertainment ready for consumption.
If you're bored, just turn on the television or pop in a video. Instant
entertainment. The problem is that we can so easily ignore the subtle
and not-so-subtle moral messages contained in such amusement.

I read a startling statistic recently. The average American
watches 1,000 hours of television a year, or about nineteen hours a
week. This means the average child has watched 18,000 hours of
television by the time she finishes high school. That's two full years,
an amazing 10 percent of her life, spent in front of television before
she reaches adulthood.

Perhaps, like me, you struggle with finding appropriate balance in all of this, especially in light of Colossians 3:1–2. This
passage exhorts us to set our minds "on things above, not on earthly
things," but the dazzling array of entertainment choices is heavy
competition for the things above.

I don't want to engage in television bashing. After all, there's
nothing wrong with wholesome entertainment. But I also don't
want to ignore the fact that the enormous number of hours spent in
front on the tube negatively impacts family after family across
America. Instead of directing your family's minds and hearts to
God, you may be unknowingly directing yourself and your children to "earthly things."

My suggestion? Cut back on television. I know it's a radical idea, but I feel it's worth consideration. Think about reducing your TV time to eight hours a week, or even four. Here are a few suggestions that might help you cut back:

• To each family member, pass out coupons for a specified number of TV hours. For each half-hour of TV a person wants to watch, she must spend one of her coupons. When the coupons are gone, no more television that week.

• If your children are old enough, hold a conference to develop family standards for acceptable TV programs. Then develop a list of programs from which your children can choose when they want to watch television.

• Provide fun, creative alternatives. My family had a reading night for a number of years. We read books out loud, including C. S. Lewis's *Narnia* series. Believe me, it was more fun than watching television.

• *Never* watch TV during mealtime.

• Don't allow your children to turn on the TV without a specific program in mind. When my kids ask me if they can watch TV, my first question is "What do you want to watch?"

• Limit using television as a baby-sitter for your preschoolers.

• Take a six-month sabbatical from television. Store your TV in a closet and see what happens.

Without realizing it, families can settle into a routine of television viewing that drains their time, prevents them from enjoying genuine fellowship together, and actually chips away at the moral values they hold dear. You don't have to let that happen in your family. Give this subject some serious thought and see where God leads you.

REFLECTIONS: Tell each other how you feel about your family's television-viewing habits. Are your minds being drawn to earthly things too often in your viewing? Do you spend too much time in front of the TV? What new guidelines would you like to put in place to revise these habits?

PRAYER FOCUS: Ask God for His perspective to see television for what it is. Pray for courage to make the decisions you need to make. Ask Him for fresh insight about how to set your minds on things above.

73
WHO IS EQUAL
TO THE TASK?

*And who is equal to such a task?... Not that we are competent
in ourselves to claim anything for ourselves,
but our competence comes from God.*

2 CORINTHIANS 2:16; 3:5

You'll agree, I think, that life presents challenge after challenge.
Sometimes there seems to be no relief from the bombardment of
tasks you must handle: that new responsibility at work, the parenting task, the ministry you've undertaken. Doubt about your ability
to meet those challenges can push its way into your mind and heart
until you feel overwhelmed. *Can I do it?* you ask yourself.

Paul, facing a job he needed to do in Macedonia, asked the
same question: "And who is equal to such a task?" Paul recognized
the enormity of the job and essentially asked, "Is this task too big
for me? Can I do the job?"

As a pastor, I meet people every day who are uncertain about
their abilities to change or grow or accomplish their tasks. I recall
one husband who listened to his wife talk about her feelings and
then said, "I will never be able to share that way. I just don't believe
I can do it."

However, a few months later, this husband was learning to
meet his wife's needs in a new way by opening up his inner world
to her. How did he do it? That question applies to every believer.
How do you make difficult personal changes? How do you grow
as a husband or wife? How do you overcome the challenges of a
new ministry and break through to success?

There's only one simple answer: *You* don't. You *and God* do.

Paul was quite clear about this, wasn't he? He said, "I know I
can't do this alone. I'm not competent enough by myself. However,

God and I can do anything! I know that with His help, we'll make this thing happen."

Overcoming the obstacles of life, moving ahead to success in whatever goal you have, will require a ton of work. But most important, it will require God working in and through you. Literally, He will give you the competence to get the job done.

How do you tap into God's adequacy? It has something to do, I think, with living in dependence upon Him. You realize your inadequacy and choose to invite God into every task. You bathe each task in prayer, asking for His wisdom. You do everything you *can* do, then ask God to do everything you *can't.*

You may face a difficult task right now in your marriage, parenting, finances, or ministry. Depend on God, understanding that your competence comes from Him. Then go for it!

REFLECTIONS: In what area(s) do you feel inadequate right now? How can you tap into God's competence?

PRAYER FOCUS: Ask God to help you know which is *your* job and which is *His.* Ask Him to make you competent to undertake the challenges you face.

74
PRESS ON

But one thing I do: Forgetting what is behind and straining toward
what is ahead, I press on toward the goal to win the prize for
which God has called me heavenward in Christ Jesus.

PHILIPPIANS 3:13–14

Do you remember the first fervor of your love for God, the excitement of knowing and serving Him? Naomi and I have clear, glowing memories of college and the first few years of marriage when we had a vivid and exciting awareness of God and what He was doing in our lives.

It's tempting to want to recapture those early memories or to remember them as high points. But Paul has a different idea in mind. He says, "forgetting what is behind and straining toward what is ahead, I press on...." Paul didn't live in the past, and neither should we. Instead, like Paul, we should press on in our Christian walk.

C. S. Lewis wrote a letter to a friend that addressed this very issue. See what you think of his words:

> Many religious people lament that the first fervors of their conversion have died away. They think—sometime rightly, but not, I believe, always—that their sins account for this. They may even try by pitiful efforts of will to revive what now seems to have been the golden days. But were those fervors—the operative word is *those*—ever intended to last?
>
> And the joke, or tragedy, of it all is that these golden moments in the past, which are so tormenting if we erect them into a norm, are entirely nourishing, wholesome,

and enchanting if we are content to accept them for what they are, for memories. Properly bedded down in a past which we do not miserably try to conjure back, they will send up exquisite growths. Leave the bulbs alone, and the new flowers will come; but hope, by fondling and sniffing, to get last year's blooms, and you will get nothing.[1]

Lewis agrees with Paul: Don't live in the past. We sometimes look back to an exciting or productive time in our spiritual walk and consider that as the norm for our lives. We want to regain the feelings from that time and so recover a sense of earlier joy and inspiration. But that's not God's design.

Lewis says it this way: "Leave the bulbs alone, and the new flowers will come." In other words, remember former times as a great gift from God, but anticipate new and different experiences to come. Let new flowers, new experiences, grow. That will happen as we live in the present and look forward to the future.

This principle holds true in the marriage relationship as well. Maybe you've hit a rough patch in your walk together. You aren't relating as closely or smoothly as you have in the past. At times like these, you may be tempted to look back on a more positive time and hold it up as the ideal, attempting to recapture it (and perhaps frustrating yourselves and each other in the process). Cherish these memories, thank God profusely for them, but don't try to recreate them. Move forward, making new memories that will keep your relationship vital.

Paul's advice? Press on. Move ahead. We serve an infinitely creative God who almost never repeats Himself. From His hand, we always have new lessons to learn, new tasks to master, new marital seasons to weather and enjoy. Instead of attempting to recapture something in the past, let God create something fresh and vibrant in the here and now.

REFLECTIONS: Have you been hanging on to memories, hoping to re-create a beautiful time from your past? How can you look to the present and future for the blessings God has for you? Can you see something specific that God wants to do in your life now and in the days to come? If so, what?

PRAYER FOCUS: Take time to thank God for what He has done for you in the past. Then ask God for excitement about the future, for a fresh vision of what He will do in and through you.

75
REFLECTIONS ON A CHANGING WORLD

Jesus Christ is the same yesterday and today and forever.

HEBREWS 13:8

Change, in big and small doses, is inevitable. I was reminded of this not too long ago by the transformation of the wooded lot behind my house. Huge machinery busily scraped, pushed, and tore away fifty years of growth. The green oasis I once knew was reduced to precisely one-half acre of dirt ready for construction. I was surprised at the emotions that swept through my heart.

This event was a graphic reminder for me that things change. Change comes in all shapes and sizes, and it can be good or bad. For example, the information age has brought the benefits of super-fast computers, cell phones, and satellite communication. In the same period, however, family breakdown and the onslaught of moral relativism have ripped through America. These and other changes seem to have torn away some of what once made us stable and secure, leaving us anxious about the future.

Maybe you've experienced some of this "future shock" and have wondered how to deal with it. As I watched the little forest behind our house being cleared, I began to reflect on how God might want us to react to change. Let me share with you a few of my musings.

First of all, I believe that change should teach us to stay close to Jesus instead of relying on this world. Nothing is permanent except God. Financial security, physical health, and social status can all change. If we hold too tightly to worldly things, we will be discontented much of the time. But Jesus will *never* change. He is the same now and forever. He's the anchor that keeps us secure when the fierce winds of change whip through our lives. As we place our primary focus on a relationship with Him, changes we face may disappoint, but they will never devastate.

Change should also alert us to potential opportunities for building God's kingdom. When a house appeared on the lot behind our house, it meant that a neighbor had moved in who needed God's love. Opportunity!

Change should motivate us to make a difference in our world. It's so tempting to sit back and feel victimized by change. But if we don't like a particular change, we can do something about it. You've probably heard the slogan, "Don't curse the darkness; light a candle." We can't do everything but we *can* do something. We can look for ways to be agents of change ourselves, not allowing our circumstances to overwhelm us.

Are you reeling from the effects of change in your life? your community? your culture? Remember that God has placed you in *this* world at *this* time for a reason. He wants to use you for His glory. As you endure the changes He allows in your life, remember that Jesus never changes. Hang on to Him, and He'll guide you through whatever mine fields of change you face. Follow Him, and you just might find yourself involved in changing things for the better.

REFLECTIONS: What changes have you recently confronted? What can you do about them? What can you learn from them? How can you find opportunity in them?

PRAYER FOCUS: Talk to God about the changes you face. Ask Him for wisdom in confronting them. Leave the burden you feel about change with Him.

76
A THREE-WAY PARTNERSHIP

Though one may be overpowered, two can defend themselves.
A cord of three strands is not quickly broken.

ECCLESIASTES 4:12

Are you partners? Yes, you're married to each other, but do you truly face life standing side by side? And as you advance through life's twists and turns together, do you invite God to actively participate in your partnership? I've noticed that when couples foster a three-way partnership with each other and their heavenly Father, they experience far fewer headaches and much more joy.

Ecclesiastes 4:12 describes an appropriate symbol for the marital union. In the ancient world, a rope was formed and strengthened by twisting together individual strands. In the same way, a couple who invite the Lord into their relationship find their lives uniquely interwoven. Each strand—husband, wife, and God Himself—combines with the others to form a strong cord that will withstand the many forces that threaten to unravel a marriage.

What are the signs that a couple view their marriage as a three-way partnership? If we used a video camera to film such a marital partnership, what would we see? First, we'd see spouses *praying* together. The camera would catch them inviting their heavenly Father to participate in their lives. When they had decisions to make, they'd call on His name. When they experienced pain or loss, they'd take that difficulty to God, asking for His strength. When they enjoyed good gifts from God, they'd express their joy to Him. The result would be obvious on film: marital roots deepening and the three-fold cord of partnership growing stronger.

What else would this videotape reveal about a marital partnership? I believe the film would show a couple *sharing* with each other and *listening* closely to each other's words. When one spouse shared an opinion or a feeling, the other would give careful attention. The couple would express their desires to each other in the sure confidence that what one partner considered important, the other would, too. They'd make decisions together in a spirited interchange of thoughts and ideas and on the altar of couple prayer. Again, the results would be obvious on film: mutual respect and a clear confidence that God would guide them as they worked together.

What final aspect of this partnership would our fictional video camera capture on film? The camera would record two people *serving* each other, shoring up any areas of weakness in each other's lives. We'd see the strengths and weaknesses of both partners complementing each other. For example, the more detail-oriented spouse might write the monthly checks. The mechanically gifted spouse might assemble the new barbecue or fix the leaky faucet. At various times throughout the week, our video would reveal two people contributing their unique strengths to each other, making the partnership stronger.

If you think your marriage is unraveling a bit, you might want to check your "cord of three strands." Together, bring your marriage before the Lord, and invite Him to strengthen your relationship as you submit it to Him.

REFLECTIONS: How would you rate yourselves in these three areas of marital partnership: praying, sharing, and listening? Are you actively inviting God to participate in your three-way partnership? PRAYER FOCUS: Invite God into your marriage again, asking Him to help you work together for a strong marital partnership.

77
DREAMING DREAMS THAT BRING GOD GLORY

We constantly pray for you…that by his power he may fulfill every
good purpose of yours and every act prompted by your faith. We pray
this so that the name of our Lord Jesus may be glorified in you.

2 THESSALONIANS 1:11–12

Are you encouraging each other to dream dreams that bring Jesus glory? You can play a key part in helping each other make a difference in people's lives.

For many years I dreamed of writing a book that would help strengthen Christian couples. I knew my dream was a long shot. For each book published in the United States each year, literally thousands are rejected by publishers. But in my spare time, I began writing a book about prayer in marriage. My wife and I enjoyed a good prayer life together, and I knew how much it had strengthened our relationship with each other and with the Lord. I wanted to encourage other couples to pursue the discipline of couple prayer, too.

Many times I felt like quitting. Whenever I neglected the project, Naomi would say something such as "I know you can do it. This is important. Go on in there and write for a while. God will open the doors at the right time." After she encouraged me this way, I'd usually tromp into the computer room and start typing another page.

Long story made short: Multnomah Publishers published *Praying with the One You Love* in 1996. Not long after that, Naomi presented me with a framed copy of the book cover with 1 Thessalonians 1:11–12 written beneath it, along with these words: "Keep dreaming dreams that bring God glory!" Every time I look at her gift I'm encouraged to "go for it."

How can you help each other make a difference for God? First, you can *encourage* each other. Again and again, in different ways, Naomi said to me, "You can do it. I'm for you. I'm behind you on this." If your spouse has a dream, something she wants to do for God, encourage her! Believe in her. Let her know that you have confidence in her.

But you can go further. You can *release* each other to minister. You see, there's always a cost involved in making a difference. Whether your partner teaches a Sunday-school class, undertakes a prayer ministry, or participates in the church drama team, her ministry may take time from you and your family. My wife never made me feel guilty about my writing. Instead, her words and attitude released me to make my dreams come true. You can do the same for each other.

Finally, you can *pray*. Just as Paul prayed that God would give the Thessalonian Christians power to fulfill every good purpose prompted by faith, so Naomi prayed for me. She asked God to be honored by my words. She asked that He would open doors for the book's publication. When I heard her prayers for me and for the book, I was encouraged to keep working for God's best. You can pray for each other, too, as you each dream your dreams.

Do you each have a dream that will bring God glory? You can take part in each other's dreams by giving three precious gifts: your encouragement, your release, and your prayers.

REFLECTIONS: Do you have dreams of honoring God? If so, share them with each other. Are you willing to encourage, release, and pray to support each other's dreams? If so, how can you do those things in the most supportive way possible?

PRAYER FOCUS: Spend a moment supporting each other's dreams in prayer. If you don't have a dream to glorify the name of Jesus, ask God to give you one.

78
COME AWAY

*Then, because so many people were coming and going
that they did not even have a chance to eat, he said to them, "Come
with me by yourselves to a quiet place and get some rest." So they
went away by themselves in a boat to a solitary place.*

MARK 6:31–32

A word from Webster's: *Hubbub (hub bub) n. an uproar; tumult.* Is
there a hubbub going on in your life right now? Are the obligations
piling up with no end in sight? At home, at work, even at church,
are things in an uproar? If so, I want to recommend Jesus' solution:
"Come with me by yourselves to a quiet place and get some rest."

"Rest," you say, "not likely! Too much to do, too little time."
I've felt the same way more than once. But I think we need to
remember the principle embedded at the center of this little story:
Rest means coming away with Jesus to a quiet place. We all need it
but find it difficult to do.

I don't think we have to wait for a yearly vacation to experience a quiet place with Jesus. In fact, I can think of several ways to
follow this principle every day.

First, find *quietness in prayer.* Actually, Jesus' words sound
almost like a definition of prayer: "Come with me by yourselves to
a quiet place." Nothing is more soothing than spending time in
prayer in a quiet place. Whether we join in prayer as couples or
spend time alone with the Lord, those moments refresh our spirits
and quiet our hearts. Time with our Lord helps us remember
Whose we are, Whom we serve, and Who empowers us.

Then seek the *quietness of couple communion.* When Naomi
and I meet at home at the end of the day, one of the best things we
can do is spend a few moments together as a couple, talking

through our day. As we share our feelings and thoughts, we find that peace starts to take hold. Why? Because it's rejuvenating to understand and be understood, to know and be known. We remember we're not alone, that someone cares deeply for us. Rather than trying to unwind by "vegging" in front of the TV, find rest and quietness together as you share healing conversation.

Don't forget to find *quietness in worship.* I can't tell you how many times I've experienced the quiet presence of God as I've worshiped Him during a church service. God doesn't accidentally or haphazardly command His children to assemble as a church and worship Him each week. He knows that as we lift our hearts in praise, we experience His presence and His sufficiency.

Finally, look for *quietness in recreation.* Recreation has the power to soothe and quiet our hearts. Somehow, when we turn from the daily grind to a totally different activity, breaking from the routine, our minds and hearts are refreshed. A bike ride in the summer sun, a long walk in the brisk fall air, a hobby, a project, a sport, or a game—all of these might take only a few short moments, but they can reward us with quiet hearts as we experience beauty or expend creative energy.

When the hubbub becomes more than you can handle, retreat to the quietness of God's presence. Don't wait for a vacation. Find a place of quietness and rest, and come away.

REFLECTIONS: Are you experiencing tumult in your life right now? How can you withdraw to a quiet place with Jesus today?
PRAYER FOCUS: Ask the Lord to help you find an appropriate balance between busyness and quietness in your lives.

79
THE GOODNESS
OF MARRIAGE

He who finds a wife finds what is good and
receives favor from the LORD.
PROVERBS 18:22

Are you aware of how much goodness you bring into each other's
lives? Can you imagine how barren your lives would be without
each other?

I was pondering these questions not too long ago when I wrote
this note to Naomi. See if these simple thoughts resonate with you.
Then, if you wish, spend some time together affirming the goodness of your own marriage.

Dear Naomi,
June 14, 1975, was a much-awaited date, wasn't it? I
remember crossing the days, weeks, and months off my calendar in eager anticipation of our wedding day. The years
since then have proved one thing to me without any doubt:
In finding you, I have found something inexpressibly good.

Think back with me for a moment to some special
memories in our marriage. No, I'm not talking about the
wonderful vacations we've had or the special anniver-
saries. Nor am I thinking of our delightful honeymoon in
Europe or even the birth of our children.

The special memories that mean so much to me are
the ones that happen every day, the memories that reveal
the goodness of our marriage relationship:

- praying together,
- words of encouragement and love,
- washing dishes together and talking about the day,

- warm hellos after a long day apart,
- our secret sharing,
- daily "I love you's,"
- handling of daily decisions with respect and affirmation,
- long gazes into each other's eyes,
- walks, smiles, and hugs.

The result of all these memories is a love that has grown each year along with respect, trust, a sense of being valued, security, warmth, and happiness. Our marriage is rock solid, in part because of these daily activities. Beyond a doubt, our marriage is good!

Somewhere in our home you have a box of poems that I have written to you over the twenty-some years we have known each other. These poems are filled with my love for you and my appreciation of all that you are and all that you have meant to me. But you know, I rarely observe you pulling those poems off the shelf and reading them once they've made it to "the box." That makes me happy, and I'll tell you why.

You must feel as I do, that the daily memories I'm talking about weave a fabric of love that brings deep satisfaction. You don't often feel the need to read those past poetic expressions because we communicate fresh declarations of love to each other every day. Daily, we write poems of love through our words and actions that help us both feel affirmed and cared for and loved.

When I found you as my wife, Naomi, I found the unmistakable goodness of marriage and the rich favor of our Lord.

REFLECTIONS: How has your marriage been good? What special memories do you have of your time together? What means the most to you about your partner?
PRAYER FOCUS: Thank God for the goodness of your marriage, naming specific qualities that you appreciate in each other.

80
THE MYTH OF
QUALITY TIME

We were gentle among you, like a mother caring for her little children.
We loved you so much that we were delighted to share with you
not only the gospel of God but our lives as well, because you had
become so dear to us.... For you know that we dealt with each of
you as a father deals with his own children.

1 THESSALONIANS 2:7–8, 11

Have you ever heard this: "I don't have a lot of time to give my kids, but I make up for it by giving them *quality* time"? Maybe you've even been tempted to buy into such an argument yourself. Before the idea takes root, allow me to debunk the myth of "quality time."

According to this myth, you can give your children most of what they need if you simply make judicious use of your time with them. So you set aside fifteen minutes here, forty-five minutes there, and plan such times so well that you accomplish a great deal more with your kids than you might otherwise.

But if you take a close look at this approach, you'll find several problems. First, kids don't cooperate. The hour you mapped out for a quality conversation just may be the time your child feels like clamming up. Teenagers, for example, may take an hour just to lower their defenses long enough to have a meaningful conversation. In order for anything approaching *quality* time to occur with your children, you need to invest *quantity* time. It's like panning for gold. If you pan enough dirt, eventually you'll see precious flecks of gold. In the same way, as a parent I must assume that I'll have to spend a lot of time with my child before the "gold" appears. Few parents hit it rich on quality time.

Second, your kids need a relationship with you, not just input from you. In the passage above, Paul writes to his spiritual children that he shared not only the gospel with them but his life as well. It's an apt description of the parenting task. Your children need you to share your life with them. They need the comfort of a consistent connection with Mom and Dad. That takes time.

One of the last things my son did before he graduated from kindergarten was make a wall plaque for me as a Father's Day gift. On the plaque was a stick figure of me with this sentence displayed in the fledgling handwriting of a six-year-old: "I love my father because he teaches me how to throw a Frisbee." Jon presented his handiwork to me with a beaming smile and a warm hug.

His plaque reminded me that I build good relationships with my children through a conglomeration of experiences through which I share my life with them. My son happened to remember the Frisbee incident because it was recent, but if such an experience were rare, reserved for "quality time," it would have quickly faded from his memory. What my son was really saying with his plaque was "I love my dad because he spends time with me."

Parenting takes time—great, prodigious, herculean amounts of time. But the results are worth the effort. Such quantities of time produce something precious indeed: close relationships with your children.

Like most parents, you have schedules to keep and deadlines to meet. You're busy. But as you plan your calendar for the weeks and months ahead, make sure to schedule in plenty of *quantity* time with your kids. As you do, you'll ensure that you'll have lots of quality time with them, too.

REFLECTIONS: How do you both feel about the time you spend with your children? Do you need to make some changes? If so, how can you implement one change in the week ahead?

PRAYER FOCUS: Ask God to help you invest your time in your family and, as you do, to give you rich times together that become cherished memories.

81
SUCCESS AND FAILURE
IN GOD'S EYES
PART ONE

You know, brothers, that our visit to you was not a failure.... With the
help of our God we dared to tell you his gospel in spite of
strong opposition. For the appeal we make does not
spring from error or impure motives.

1 THESSALONIANS 2:1–3

Ever felt like a failure, like you just weren't reaping the results you wanted in a relationship or ministry in which you were involved? You're not alone.

It's easy to be confused about what true success is. As a pastor, I've sometimes felt the dull ache of failure. At such times, I've needed God's perspective in evaluating my performance.

Paul's words in 1 Thessalonians 2:1–3 give us a new standard by which to measure our success, whether we are relating to our spouses, working with other believers to build God's kingdom, or ministering to our neighbors about Jesus. The apostle Paul was not a man to mince words or sugarcoat a difficult truth. You'll never find him putting a good face on a bad situation. So when he says that his time in Thessalonica was *not* a failure, he meant it. Paul's words have helped me redefine success and failure, especially as they apply to relationships and service to others. Perhaps they'll help you, too.

Paul says he was not a failure in Thessalonica. Why? First, because he was willing to minister despite the cost. When Paul arrived in Thessalonica, he encountered strong opposition. We don't know how that manifested itself, but it certainly meant pain for him. When believers encounter difficulty in ministry, most want to draw back, even hide. Instead, Paul dared to minister despite the pain. He didn't give up or shrink back. He kept trying.

Now get this: God calls that success. When we're willing to keep giving our best and to keep moving ahead in the process, God says, "That's success."

A second standard helped Paul measure success. "I know I wasn't a failure," Paul says, "because what I told you was the truth." You may not be able to predict how others will respond to the truth, but you can always speak the truth in love. Sometimes we're tempted to skew our words about Jesus because we're thinking about the listener's reaction. Instead of telling the truth, we say what we think the other person wants to hear.

Certainly we should be wise and loving about what we say and when we say it, but when we speak God's truth, we give something of real value. Anything less springs from an impure motive. Our spouses, co-workers, and neighbors may not always respond to the truth immediately, but we have God's assurance that speaking the truth is one measure of success in His eyes.

You might be tempted to give up right now on a relationship or worthwhile endeavor because you just don't see the results you want. Perhaps you have your own picture of success and haven't reached it yet. As a result, you're doubting yourself and your efforts. Is it possible that God wants to change your view of success? Do you need to reassess your efforts?

REFLECTIONS: Describe to each other a relationship or ministry task that feels like a failure to you right now. Help each other see how you might really be successful in God's eyes.

PRAYER FOCUS: Pray for clear vision about what success really means. Ask God to help you persevere in your present situation with renewed commitment.

82
SUCCESS AND FAILURE
IN GOD'S EYES
PART TWO

Our visit to you was not a failure.... For the appeal we make does not spring from error or impure motives, nor are we trying to trick you.... We are not trying to please men but God, who tests our hearts. You know we never used flattery, nor did we put on a mask to cover up greed—God is our witness....we were gentle among you, like a mother caring for her little children. We loved you so much.
1 THESSALONIANS 2:1, 3–5, 7–8

"Our visit was not a failure," Paul said. Why wasn't it a failure? What made his visit a success in God's eyes? Understanding Paul's success can help us determine what God deems successful in our lives, too. So let's dissect Paul's example and learn from it.

First, we're successful in God's eyes when we minister without manipulation. The word "trick" in the 1 Thessalonians passage has the connotation of catching a fish by means of bait. It's sometimes tempting to tell a half-truth, feign ignorance, flatter, or even aggressively pressure someone to do as we wish. Even if we have good intentions, as in ministering to people, manipulation isn't honest and has the powerful potential to backfire.

Paul didn't do that; instead he was straightforward. Regardless of the results, God says success has to do with our forthright approach with people. Do we speak honestly and relate with integrity? Do we put others' interests ahead of our own? If we do, God identifies us as successful.

Another standard that puts us in the winner's circle in God's eyes has to do with motive, *why* we do what we do. Paul said his motive was to please God, not men. I've felt intense pressure more than once to act with a particular person's pleasure in mind, rather than God's. Instead of doing the right thing, trusting that God will use it, I've been tempted to placate or appease.

Finally, God's idea of success requires love. Do we act out of greed for our own good, or do we choose to minister out of love? Paul's description of his love for the Thessalonians is a good example: "We were gentle among you, like a mother caring for her little children." What could be a more tender expression of love than that of a mother with her children? Love is primarily a choice, not a feeling, and choosing to love others is a way we can always be successful in God's eyes.

"What about results?" you might ask. What about the tangible evidence that indicates success? Obviously, we always welcome positive results, but remember, believers sometimes find it hard to evaluate results from *God's* perspective. What we might call failure may actually warm our Father's heart.

Have you been discouraged recently? Maybe you need to recommit yourself to action that will please the Lord, regardless of how others respond. Perhaps you need to reevaluate the situation, looking at it from God's perspective.

REFLECTIONS: How well do your views of success match with Paul's words in this passage? Do you put pressure on yourself that doesn't need to be there? How can you pursue God's view of success today?

PRAYER FOCUS: Ask God to help you see success from His perspective.

83
MAKING JESUS THE
CENTER OF YOUR HOME

Unless the LORD builds the house, its builders labor in vain.
Unless the LORD watches over the city,
the watchmen stand guard in vain.

PSALM 127:1

I value hard work, and sometimes I'm tempted to believe it's the key to almost everything. That includes, of course, a fabulous family life. Just get in there and make it happen—that's my attitude. As husband and father, it's so easy to believe that I'm in charge, that my family is totally in my hands.

Psalm 127:1 provides a reality check for such an attitude: "Unless the LORD builds the house, its builders labor in vain." In other words, all my efforts amount to nothing if God isn't involved. Unless my family and I acknowledge His place at the center of our home, we're in big trouble. Period. Without that attitude, we "labor in vain."

So, how do you make Jesus the center of your home? How do you acknowledge Him as the unseen builder of your household? I suspect that specific answers vary from family to family. In examining my own family life, three thoughts come to mind.

First, as a family we acknowledge our dependence upon God. This happens in all kinds of ways. When we thank God for our food at mealtimes, we're saying, "We know that You have provided for us, that we're dependent upon Your goodness." We also pray together at day's end. During a recent family prayer time, our children were thinking about the first day of school just around the corner. It was the perfect time to pray together, each of us asking our Father to give His help during the coming school year. What were we saying? "Going to school without You would be in vain.

We're dependent upon You."

Second, our family tries to acknowledge His continuous presence among us. We live knowing that He is with us in our work, in our amusements, and in our conversations. We try to remember that He is always with us, sitting at the dinner table or riding with us in the car. We want to live life in light of His presence.

So, for example, we try to evaluate our speech based on His presence. We ask ourselves, "Would these words please Jesus?" When we rent a video, we ask ourselves, "Can we invite the Lord to watch this with us?" When a need arises, we're learning to pray first, knowing that God is indeed *with* us, that He is relevant to our lives, that He'll answer our call.

Finally, we try to acknowledge His rule in our home. When we have decisions to make, we know we can and should turn to Him first. When our oldest daughter was recently considering where to go to college, we bowed together in prayer, trusting that God would give us His wisdom. We also try to trust Him through life's white water. When God has allowed our family to experience pain, we've assailed the gates of heaven with prayer and have rested in His sovereignty. In these and other ways, we've acknowledged God as our divine watchman.

What about your home? Do you place God firmly at the center? Brick by brick, work with Him to build a home where you honor Him as Lord. As you do, you'll succeed in building a healthy, joyful family.

PRAYER FOCUS: No discussion today. Simply dedicate or rededicate your home to God. Invite Him to be the center of your home, and ask Him for the wisdom and strength to serve Him as Lord each day.

84
OVERCOMING ANXIETY

*Do not be anxious about anything, but in everything, by prayer
and petition, with thanksgiving, present your requests to God.
And the peace of God, which transcends all understanding,
will guard your hearts and your minds in Christ Jesus.*

PHILIPPIANS 4:6–7

I was amused some time ago when a friend decided to help his wife
with her worry problem. My peaceful friend told his worried wife
that she could rest easy. "From now on," he said, "I'll do the worrying for both of us." Her instant retort was significant: "Yes," she
said, "but you don't worry right!"

For the Christian, there's no "right way" to worry. In fact,
Philippians 4:6–7 urges us not to worry at all. This passage assures
us that whatever happens in our lives, our marriages, or our families, we don't have to waste time worrying about it. This doesn't
mean we shouldn't be concerned about a problem or avoid thinking about solutions. It does mean that the nonproductive fretting of
an anxious heart is not God's plan for His kids.

Believe me, we can't escape problems. Some years ago Dr.
Thomas Holmes of the University of Washington designed a test
to measure the level of stress in one's life. The test assigns various
point values to specific life events according to how much potential
stress might accompany those events. For example, trouble with in-
laws is assigned a moderate point value. Pregnancy is high on the
stress scale. Even moving out of your house, according to Dr.
Holmes, produces stress. And anything that brings stress into our
lives can also worry us.

When worry gets a grip on us, producing that gnawing feeling
in the stomach, we can help ourselves out of it by understanding

how anxiety works. Anxiety starts on the inside and works outward. In other words, worry has more to do with a person's *assessment* of a situation than with the situation itself. Our responses to life's potential stressors are first internal—how we evaluate whatever problem we face. That internal monologue affects our reactions and can easily lead us to worry.

When we realize that worry is working its way into our mindset, what can we do to counteract it? Pray. One of the best things any couple can do to resist anxiety is to pray individually and as a couple. Prayer says, "I trust You, Father." Isn't it great that we can take our needs and burdens to the One who loves us and leave them there? Philippians 4:6–7 even links thankful prayer to God's peace, for when we pray, we sense the heavenly Father's powerful presence and know that He will help. Suddenly the burden is no longer ours but God's, and we can rest in that truth.

There's always plenty to worry about, isn't there? You may have a worrisome situation intruding into your life right now, and you're fighting fretfulness and anxiety. This time, do something different. Take your needs to your Father and allow Him to give you His peace as you join together in prayer.

REFLECTIONS: What kinds of things tempt you to worry? Is there something going on in your life right now that is causing anxiety? If so, what?

PRAYER FOCUS: First, join together and pray for any problem you currently face. Then ask God to help you consistently choose prayer over worry.

85
SEXUAL SATISFACTION

Drink water from your own cistern.... May your fountain be blessed,
and may you rejoice in the wife of your youth. A loving doe,
a graceful deer—may her breasts satisfy you always,
may you ever be captivated by her love.

PROVERBS 5:15, 18–19

No doubt about it: God wants you to have a satisfying sexual relationship. Proverbs 5, together with a number of other biblical passages, depicts the sexual relationship between a husband and wife as good and as a source of genuine pleasure. In fact, Proverbs 5:19 counsels husbands to be "captivated" by the love of their wives. "Captivated" means exhilarated or intoxicated, the emotional thrill associated with the sexual adventure. Such words affirm that sexuality is God's gift to us and that we can receive it with pleasure.

"Okay," one might respond, "but how?" I could offer a number of suggestions here, but I'll underscore an important issue this passage raises. It's called fidelity, also known as faithfulness, loyalty, or even devotion. When the writer says, "Drink water from your own cistern" and "rejoice in the wife of your youth," he means one thing: Do whatever it takes to remain true to the one you love. Year after year, let your spouse be your only source of sexual pleasure, but even more, continually maintain your entire relationship, taking joy in the marital union.

Of course, this goes against society's message, which is "If excitement is dwindling in the relationship, just get a new model." You're aware, as I am, of forty-five-year-old men who dump their wives and marry twenty-year-olds. How does this happen? Doubtless, every tale is different, but it begins when spouses stop putting energy and attention into their relationship. It continues as the sexual experience becomes less than satisfying. It ends with one or both spouses concluding that happiness depends on finding another sexual partner.

I'm going to tell you something you probably already know. The best way to kill a good sex life is to start ignoring the relationship as a whole. Authors Ed and Gaye Wheat make this claim: "A couple cannot separate sex from the rest of the marriage...everything that happens in the marriage has its effect upon the lovemaking experience."[1] A woman, especially, tends to view her sexual experience in terms of the total relationship. She wants to feel loved and cherished as a person. When her husband is sensitive to her emotional and spiritual needs, she is more sexually responsive. She wants what some have called "all-day lovemaking," a feeling that her husband loves her in various ways all day long. A man benefits from such constant reassurance of his wife's love too.

An updated and inclusive paraphrase of the Proverbs 5 passage might read something like this: "Give your emotional and sexual energy only to each other. Keep taking joy in the marriage, choosing to maintain the relationship with the one you married so long ago. Let your love find a way to keep the sexual spark alive so that you are attracted to your partner. In fact, revel in the joy of sexual pleasure. Let your love be a top priority."

How can you fulfill these words in your marriage today?

REFLECTIONS: Have you found ways to keep your sexual relationship fresh and vibrant? What do you do to maintain all areas of your relationship so that your sexual bond benefits?

PRAYER FOCUS: Pray for a renewed devotion to your entire relationship, including sustained sexual satisfaction.

86
WHAT "NOT" TO SAY TO YOUR CHILDREN

Parents, do not treat your children in such
a way as to make them angry.
EPHESIANS 6:4 (TEV)

What messages do you communicate to your children? What do they hear from you day in and day out? The messages you send to your kids are important because children tend to believe what you tell them. That's especially true of messages they hear often, whether directly by your words or indirectly by your attitude or actions. If you don't carefully evaluate what you say to your children, you may run the risk of hardening your children's hearts. The advice of Ephesians 6:4 is clear: Don't let your words and actions make your children angry, ultimately crushing their hearts and leaving them discouraged.

What messages do we want to avoid giving our children? They fall into four categories.

1. "You're bad" I saw a young parent with an active preschooler in the grocery store recently. The little boy had unscrewed the cap on a shampoo bottle and had poured the shampoo into the shopping cart. Not good by any parental standard, but judging by the mother's reaction you'd have thought this child had robbed a bank. His mother said something I hadn't heard in years. "BAD boy," she scolded. "BAD boy." Want to embitter your children? Just communicate to them that they're bad or insensitive or stupid. Any of a thousand variations on "you're bad" will sink deep into a child's heart.

2. "I wish you were different." This conveys the message "I'm disappointed in you." A typical way to communicate this message goes something like this: "Why can't you be like your brother?"

Sometimes parents communicate this about unchangeable physical characteristics such as a child's height, build, or even gender. This says to the child, "I don't accept you as you are." Believe me, such a message will send a child into the world insecure and anxious.

3. *"You're not important."* Parents usually communicate this message more by what they *don't* do than what they do. Lack of parental involvement says one thing to a child: "You're not important." Children understand that their parents need to make a living. However, when they see their parents make choices with discretionary time that exclude them again and again, they feel left out and unimportant.

4. *"My love for you is linked to your performance."* Perhaps one of the most damaging messages a parent can communicate to a child is that the child is not loved. This often happens when the parent expresses disappointment about the child's performance. Ideally, parents should communicate this message to their kids: "I love you just the way you are, no matter how you perform." Yet parents can subtly communicate conditional love to a son or daughter based on the child's performance. The result? Either the child gives up and rebels against the parents, knowing he or she can never please them, or the child becomes dependent upon them in unhealthy ways. Either response produces an angry heart in a child who feels unloved.

I know you're doing the best job you can of raising your children. You love them with all your heart. Since you do, fill their minds and hearts with messages of love, acceptance, and worth, and they'll go into the world confident and secure.

REFLECTIONS: Honestly evaluate the messages you send your children. Are the messages positive ones? Is there one area in which you could do better?

PRAYER FOCUS: Thank God for your children. Ask Him to empower you to communicate positive messages that will encourage your kids.

87
MAINTAINING YOUR SPIRITUAL ROOTS

*So then, just as you received Christ Jesus as Lord, continue to live
in him, rooted and built up in him, strengthened in the faith
as you were taught, and overflowing with thankfulness.*

COLOSSIANS 2:6–7

You live in the real world. You've felt the tension between the demands of this world and the importance of maintaining your relationship with Christ. Priorities push and pull and tug until you feel you have no time for what's *most* important—a vital friendship with God.

Paul's gentle encouragement to the Colossians rings true for us today: There's a big difference between *receiving* Christ Jesus and *continuing* to live in Him. The former is an event; the latter is a process and a lifelong adventure. This passage from Colossians provides a visual image to encourage believers as we build our spiritual lives. It's the picture of a plant, perhaps in the midst of a garden, its roots sinking deeply into the good earth.

You don't have to be a horticulturist to understand that healthy plants need nurturing. For a plant to bear the maximum fruit possible, it must have care. Planting is only the beginning. In the Northwest, where I live, slugs will decimate tomato plants unless you somehow protect your plants from them. You not only have to guard against pests, but you also regularly have to pull weeds, fertilize and water your plants, and make sure they get enough sun. And if you want the greatest harvest, you have to pick the fruit so that more will grow.

The result of such care is a plant whose roots sink deep, a healthy plant that continues to bear fruit.

Of course, maintenance is a time drain, no doubt about it. But you do receive something in return: healthy plants and a productive garden. Have you ever planted a garden then neglected to care for it? I have. Soon my garden was choked with weeds and wilted from lack of water. On the other hand, you may have also felt the satisfaction of growing a garden in which plants were firmly rooted in deep, rich soil, where your care resulted in green and healthy living things.

A growing relationship with God takes maintenance too. I learned long ago that believers choose just how close they'll be to God by the daily decisions they make to nurture that relationship. We alone determine how intimate we are with God. We make our own choices about whether we'll "continue to live in him, rooted and built up in him." Points of contact with God such as prayer, Bible reading, and meditation take time, but they deepen our spiritual roots as nothing else does.

Molding a close relationship with God is a lifelong journey, but it's worth the effort. Perhaps you've known someone who has maintained a growing relationship with God. You've sensed the joy, the love, and the peace. You've seen the fruit. All are the result of "continuing to live in him, rooted and built up in him."

Next time you water or fertilize your garden, remember to take some time to maintain your relationship with God, too.

REFLECTIONS: Be completely honest with each other about your level of spiritual intimacy with God. Are you maintaining your relationship with Him? Do you feel close to Him? What could you do to better maintain your spiritual life?

PRAYER FOCUS: Invite God into an intimate relationship with you. Pray for a realignment of priorities so that you can grow closer to Him.

88
THE GIVING PRINCIPLE

*"Give, and it will be given to you. A good measure, pressed down,
shaken together and running over, will be poured into your lap.
For with the measure you use, it will be measured to you."*

LUKE 6:38

Want a principle that will absolutely revolutionize your marriage?
Here it is: "Give, and it will be given to you." This overarching
principle can work in every area of your lives, including your marriage. When you give to each other, that gift will not only
accomplish something good for your spouse, it will guarantee that
something good will return to you as well.

Let me tell you a tale I heard long ago. I'm not sure if it's a true
story, but if it isn't, it ought to be. A man went to his lawyer saying
that he wanted to divorce his wife. "She treats me terribly," he said,
"and I just want out." The lawyer devised a plan. "Why not spend
the next three months saying and doing everything you can to
make her feel loved? Then, just when her feelings for you have
revived, stick her with the divorce papers. It will devastate her."
The man went home and did exactly that, lavishing his wife with
acts of love and kindness. But by the end of the three months, his
wife was treating him so well, he decided to forget the divorce and
go on a second honeymoon instead!

Self-giving love is hard to resist. If you give it, you are virtually
guaranteed to receive it in return.

The truth is that people tend to reciprocate what they receive.
If you speak kind words to your wife, she will tend to speak kind
words back. If you regularly demonstrate caring behavior to your
husband, he will probably want to reciprocate with care in return.
You are the biggest factor in determining what will happen in your

marriage. Each of you holds tremendous power in helping your partner respond positively in your relationship.

Consider the difference between a thermometer and a thermostat. A thermometer can only measure the temperature around it. It has no power to make a change of any kind. However, you can use a thermostat to actually set the temperature you want. Some people experience marriage as thermometers. They measure the emotional and relational temperature around them but feel powerless to make any positive changes. Others see themselves as thermostats. They set the positive emotional and relational temperature by what they say and do, knowing their partners will respond to their words and actions. They understand that whatever they give will be given back to them.

Are there marriages in which this doesn't work? Sure. In severely conflicted marriages, one or both partners may harden their hearts to the other, becoming completely unwilling to give. However, it takes a long time to get to that point. Even in such a case, the truth of the Scripture still applies. Your positive acts of giving will always result in something good returning to you. Perhaps it will be the development of your own character or a closer dependence upon God. Either way, a "good measure, pressed down, shaken together and running over" will be poured into your life.

What are you waiting for? What can you give your spouse today? Affection? Completion of a task that will make life easier for him? A kind word? Give, and give freely, knowing that when you give, you can't lose.

REFLECTIONS: Affirm each other by pointing out three ways in which your partner gives to you regularly. Then share how these acts of giving make you feel.

PRAYER FOCUS: Pray for a giving heart and for a marriage in which you give to each other regularly.

89
FAMILY HARMONY

If a house is divided against itself, that house cannot stand.

MARK 3:25

Over the years you've undoubtedly observed families in trouble. Divorce, rebellion, and discord have toppled some of those families, ripping through households with hurricane force. Maybe you've wondered, "How in the world can we make sure something like that doesn't happen to us?"

There are no easy answers, but Mark 3:25 suggests an important concept for maintaining family harmony. It simply says that a family cannot stand if it's divided against itself. In other words, unless conflict is resolved, a family will ultimately self-destruct.

Conflict is inevitable in every family and in every marriage. It's simply what happens when people disagree. It *will* happen; the only question is *how* the family will handle it. Will family members avoid it? Will one member of the family try to win, regardless of the cost to others? Will some family members ignore the needs of other members?

For a family to live in harmony, parents and children must have good ways of handling conflict. Over the years, I've noticed that harmonious families have two characteristics in common: They listen well, and they talk often. Sounds so simple, doesn't it? Believe me, these two choices can go a long way toward bringing harmony to your home.

Listening is a major asset in handling conflict, but you'd be surprised how seldom families use it. One family member speaks; another interrupts. They fight to get their points across. Comments begin to fly without much thought. When this happens, the process resembles a sparring match, with each person giving and receiving a series of quick punches.

There's a great alternative: listening! Listening means hearing the content and emotion of someone's words so well that you can accurately paraphrase them. In fact, you help each other when you do just that. For example, "I'm hearing that you're angry because I didn't include you in this decision. Is that right?" or "Sounds like you're pretty serious about this new job." Misunderstandings happen far less frequently when you listen to each other. Instead of offering an immediate emotional response, you really hear what another person says and communicate your understanding.

When people feel listened to, they tend to calm down and start listening in return. Friction decreases, and family members begin trying to understand each other. Families who listen to each other avoid the divisions that can bring them down.

Of course, talking is important too. Clamming up makes conflict resolution pretty tough. Sharing thoughts and feelings can make all the difference in the world. Parents who encourage conversation at all levels set the pace for their kids. In addition, parents who offer a few well-placed questions and then a listening ear often find their kids opening up to them.

Want to maintain your family's unity? Want to ensure that harmony is the norm? Learn to listen and talk, and teach your children to do the same. Head off division before it poisons your family.

REFLECTIONS: Evaluate your family's communication skills. Do you listen and talk to each other? Is there harmony in your home? What can you do to move even closer?

PRAYER FOCUS: Pray for harmony in your home. Ask God to help all family members listen to each other and learn to share what they think and feel.

90
SUBMISSION: IS IT OLD-FASHIONED?

Wives, in the same way be submissive to your husbands.

1 PETER 3:1

The issue of wifely submission has to be one of the hottest topics of the past decade or so. It has led to a lot of debate and hostility.

You've probably heard the various positions espoused by both sides in the debate. Have you felt a bit confused by it all? Have you wondered what all the fuss is about?

Let's cut through some of the misunderstandings and come to the practical heart of the matter. First, we must know what the term "submission" does *not* mean. Submission has nothing to do with what I call the "1940s" view of marriage. You're probably familiar with this view. Some quarters still teach it today. In this view, a wife must be docile and passive. When her husband speaks, she must never question his decisions. She's essentially his lieutenant, and he's the captain. The husband holds all the power in the relationship, and if he chooses to abuse that power, so be it. After all, the wife must submit.

I'll never forget a true story I read several years ago that illustrates this 1940s view of marriage. A man was visiting a family and noticed something strange. Every time he talked to the wife, she looked at her husband before answering. Finally, the visitor asked her what was going on. She replied, "Through some teaching we've heard recently, we've realized that I am to submit to my husband. We decided that true submission means that I should gain permission from my husband before speaking in public."

Talk about a misunderstanding!

One hundred and eighty degrees from this view is something called egalitarianism. While the egalitarian relationship is far closer to the biblical view of marriage, it, too, demonstrates a misunderstanding of submission's true meaning. According to this view, God intends for a husband and wife to be exactly equal in every way, including the roles they play in marriage. In other words, a husband and wife are co-leaders of the family. There is, therefore, no "head of the household."

This is a nice view, but there's a problem with it: It's not God's plan.

The biblical view of marriage, one that takes into account the submission issue, is *equal partnership with a designated head.* Certainly husbands and wives are equal in personhood, intelligence, gifting, and spirituality. However, in God's sovereignty, He has given the husband the additional responsibility of being the designated head of the marriage partnership. It has nothing to do with superiority, only with the role that God has given him.

In such a marriage, intellectual interaction should be the norm. A husband and wife should respect each other and listen to each other's perspectives. Key decisions should drive couples to their knees together, seeking God's best. However, submission means that if a couple must make a decision and they can't reach an agreement about it, a wife must ultimately trust her husband's final say-so.

Submission has to do with a wife's voluntary support of her husband's leadership. In my own marriage, I look on my leadership role as a responsibility, not a privilege. It means that I must extend self-sacrificing love to Naomi. She in turn submits to such love. In the context of mutual submission, we work out the roles that God has assigned to each of us.

This is a difficult subject, but one on which couples need to agree. What about you? Have you worked out the submission issue in your own marriage?

REFLECTIONS: What's your view of submission? How do you work it out in your relationship? Do you need to make any changes? If so, what?

PRAYER FOCUS: Ask God to give you unity in the areas of submission and leadership within your relationship.

91
THE AWESOME POWER
OF GIVING THANKS

And be filled with thanksgiving.
COLOSSIANS 2:7 (TEV)

Do you live life in a constant state of thankfulness? Hard question, isn't it? We know that Colossians 2:7 and other Scriptures encourage us to give thanks, even to overflow with thankfulness, but the secret of such an attitude seems elusive.

I won't ask you to slip on your rose-colored glasses during the next few minutes, but I do want to help you discover the awesome power of giving thanks.

God commands His kids to be filled with thanksgiving. Why? First, because giving thanks inspires us to faith and trust. When we begin to remember who God is and what He has done in the past, we're encouraged to look beyond our present difficulties and trust God.

More than once, I have had to spend money on unexpected automobile repairs. Can you relate? I never like to hear a mechanic say, "You need a new transmission." Anxiety, panic, and discouragement are all options in such a situation. At such times, however, I'm learning to remember God's goodness and all the times He has provided for me in the past. Soon, I'm praising Him for His faithfulness. Instead of feeling discouraged, I'm inspired to trust my Lord. *After all,* I think, *God's in charge. He'll get me through.*

Thankful hearts fill us with hope, the confident expectation that God will take care of us.

Without hope, life is bleak. In Lamentations 3:19–20, the writer almost lets his circumstances drag him under: "I remember my affliction and my wandering, the bitterness and the gall....and my soul is downcast within me." The writer wallows in self-pity and loses hope.

But look what happens when this same writer decides to give thanks: "Yet this I call to mind and therefore I have hope: Because of the LORD's great love…his compassions never fail. They are new every morning…" (Lamentations 3:21–23). As the writer remembers who God is, hope returns. That's the awesome power of giving thanks.

Finally, giving thanks helps us succeed. When we complain, when we tell ourselves what a terrible fix we're in, our minds dwell on why our circumstances are so bad, why possible solutions won't work, and why things can never be all right again. When we remember all that God has done in the past, however, and when we give thanks to Him in the present, we're filled with hope and trust. That's when our minds are open to the solutions God has for us. Hopelessness saps our strength and serves to filter out solutions. Thankfulness, on the other hand, keeps us open to the possibilities.

Don't curse your hurts. Don't nurse them. Don't rehearse them. No situation is so bleak that God's grace can't shine through. Giving thanks to your Father regardless of the circumstances will remind you how big God is and how small your problems are in comparison.

Do dark clouds seem to obscure God's presence in your life right now? Are you stuck in a cycle of bitterness or self-pity? Break out with praise. Discover the awesome power of giving thanks.

REFLECTIONS: Are you facing a difficult circumstance right now? Can you express thankfulness in the midst of that difficulty?

PRAYER FOCUS: No requests today. Instead, spend time remembering God's goodness in all the areas of your life, then thank Him for who He is and what He has done.

92
TAKING RISKS

"'Master,' he said, 'I knew that you are a hard man, harvesting where
you have not sown and gathering where you have not scattered seed.
So I was afraid and went out and hid your talent in the ground. See,
here is what belongs to you.' His master replied, 'You wicked, lazy ser-
vant!... You should have put my money on deposit with the bankers, so
that when I returned I would have received it back with interest.'"
MATTHEW 25:24–27

Have you experienced a time in your married life or as individuals when God has asked you to take a risk? Maybe He has called you to step into a new ministry at your church, or perhaps He has challenged you to give money to a certain missions project. You want to please God, but stepping out in faith feels uncomfortable, risky.

The parable of the talents told by Jesus in Matthew 25 has a lot to say about this kind of situation. You know the story. Before going away, a master deposited varying amounts of money with three of his servants. He wanted each of his servants to put his money to work so that it would produce something more. The first two servants invested wisely and gained a profit by the time their master came home. The last servant, however, hid his money in the ground, and upon the master's return, had nothing to show for it. The passage above shows the master's reaction—he was not pleased!

This parable has always interested me because it clearly pictures the number-one obstacle to faith and to taking the risks necessitated by faith. The servant refused to risk because he was afraid of the possible losses. Sound familiar? I don't know about you, but what most often prevents me from moving out in faith is the *fear of failure.* I ask myself, *What if this doesn't work? What will people say? How will I recover from the loss?* As a result, I find it all too easy to hide my "talent" in the ground and refuse to take a risk.

God doesn't want us to take the talents, money, and resources He has provided and stick them in the ground. He wants us to overcome our fear of failure and make the faith investments which He asks of us.

Naturally, those investments will vary. Maybe the Lord wants you to take the relatively small risk of asking a coworker to go to church with you. Or perhaps He's asking you to take a bigger risk. I have a friend who is taking a leave of absence from his business and taking his family on a three-month missions project during the upcoming year. Is this a risk? Sure. But it's an investment he and his family believe Jesus wants them to make.

"What if I fail?" you may ask. The only way you'll fail is if you refuse to set goals and take risks; that is, if you hide your talents in the ground. Ask God what "investments" He wants you to make to build His kingdom. You might be surprised at what you hear. Go on—take a risk!

REFLECTIONS: Has God been speaking to you individually or as a couple about a faith venture? What risk does He want you to take? Is anything holding you back? If so, what? How can you get past those obstacles to take the risk God asks of you?

PRAYER FOCUS: Ask for eyes of faith to see the "investments" He wants you to make in the months ahead and then for boldness in stepping out and taking the risk.

93
HELLOS AND GOOD-BYES

Greet one another with a kiss of love.

1 PETER 5:14

Among your most important moments together every day are ones to which you may have given little thought: your hellos and good-byes. These seemingly insignificant three minutes or so—the time it takes to say hello and good-bye each day—have tremendous power to affirm and support the one you love. Obviously, these moments won't make or break your marriage, but they will make a difference in your feelings of closeness to one another on a day-to-day basis.

I'm intrigued by the fact that Peter instructed believers to "greet one another with a kiss of love." Apparently, this was a practice in the early church that communicated mutual respect and love in the Lord. What intrigues me about this verse is the significance Peter places on the greeting itself. It's important, he said, to use that beginning contact with another believer to express love. Applied to marriage, this verse certainly suggests the importance of paying attention to your hellos and good-byes.

I can hear someone saying, "This is ridiculous. What difference does it make?" I was recently reminded of how important it is in my own marriage. I'm a hugger and usually greet Naomi warmly after we've been apart. Often this greeting turns into a conversation about our day. Over the past summer, however, when I came home from work, Naomi often seemed occupied with making dinner or talking on the phone. Sometimes I wanted to change my clothes immediately and get to work on a project. Without thinking about it, for several weeks I got out of the habit of approaching her immediately with a hug and kiss when I came home. Near the end of the summer, she said to me, "Art, why haven't you been greeting me when you come home and saying good-bye before you leave? I've been missing your hugs."

Small things can make a big difference.

Naomi and I have been married a long while. She knows I love her with all my heart. However, after just a few weeks of missing hellos and good-byes, she experienced a sense of loss. Though she knew I loved her, my failure to make significant contact with her at these important times reduced her feelings of connectedness with me. I was sending an unintended message of indifference.

Attending to the crucial few minutes around your hellos and good-byes will communicate one message: "You're important to me." Your warm hellos will help you to stay connected emotionally; your tender good-byes will affirm your love for your partner.

Have you forgotten this basic principle in your marriage? Have harried schedules and preoccupation erased these important moments from your day? Small things can make such a difference. Focus on these few moments each day in your own marriage, and you'll discover how crucial they can be.

REFLECTIONS: Do you receive each other's full attention when you come together as well as when you're about to part company? If not, would you like to? What can you do to make good use of those precious moments?

PRAYER FOCUS: Pray for an even greater awareness of what will make your partner feel loved and important when you greet and when you say good-bye.

94
WHEN YOU'RE AWAY

*For I want very much to see you, in order to share a spiritual
blessing with you to make you strong.*

ROMANS 1:11 (TEV)

I'm writing this one from a hotel room. I'm away at a denomina-
tional conference and must confess that I miss my wife and family.
And this has me thinking: How do you stay close to the one you
love even when you're apart?

I'm sure you understand what I'm feeling; you've been there.
Inevitably, couples experience times of separation. A business trip,
a retreat, an emergency, or an opportunity can separate husbands
and wives for a weekend, a week, or even longer.

Three words from Scripture provide an active strategy that
can help keep your relationship strong even when you're apart.

1. Remember. Paul said to the Philippians, "I thank my God
every time I remember you" (Philippians 1:3). What a simple principle. When apart, think of each other every day and remember
something in each other for which you're grateful. What a great
way to keep your affections strongly centered on the one you love.
If you want to go even further, keep a journal while you're apart,
writing down your partner's traits for which you are especially
thankful. Then present your journals to each other when you're
together again.

2. Pray. Listen to Colossians 4:12: "Epaphras...is always
wrestling in prayer for you, that you may stand firm in all the will
of God, mature and fully assured." While separated from the
church at Colossae, Epaphras did the only thing he could do for
this church: He prayed. Although he couldn't be with his friends,
he could touch the heart of God for the ones he loved.

In the same way, you can do something positive for each other while you're apart: You can pray. I'll tell you a secret. You'll reap tremendous benefits when you pray for each other, in addition to what God will do through your prayers. When you pray for each other, you invest in each other; when you make an investment, your heart tends to stay connected to that investment. Praying for each other when you're physically apart will keep you emotionally attached.

Let me suggest that before your time of separation, you ask each other for prayer concerns. Then, when you're reunited, ask each other what God has done, and rejoice together.

3. Watch. Galatians 6:1 says, "But watch yourself, or you also may be tempted." While this can apply to the one who stays home, it applies especially to the one who's away. Frankly, there are dangers on the road. You're alone. No one knows what you're doing. You're more vulnerable. Temptation, especially sexual temptation, may try to gnaw its way through your spiritual defenses.

Yielding to temptation will not only break fellowship with God but also separate you from the one you love. To avoid these temptations, "watch yourself." Be alert to spiritual danger, and do whatever it takes to guard your heart. Be proactive. Call each other frequently and talk about your day. Pray together over the phone; it will help you stay close. Staying connected spiritually will make all the difference in keeping your affections firmly centered on each other.

Want to stay close when you're apart? Keep these three words in mind: remember, pray, and watch.

Now, please excuse me. It's time for me to pick up the phone and call my wife.

PRAYER FOCUS: No discussion today; just pray together. Ask God for closeness at all times and for special grace to keep you connected when you're apart.

95
LIFE IS HARD, BUT GOD IS GOOD

Though the fig tree does not bud and there are no grapes on the vines....
yet I will rejoice in the LORD, I will be joyful in God my Savior.
The Sovereign LORD is my strength; he makes my feet like
the feet of a deer, he enables me to go on the heights.

HABAKKUK 3:17–19

Have you ever heard the saying "Life is hard, and then you die"? Although it makes me smile, I don't really relate to such fatalism. While we all endure difficulties at times, I've found that God's goodness abounds through it all.

I propose a new saying: "Life is hard, but God is good."

I think Habakkuk would agree with me. In verses 17–19, he declares a truth no believer wants to think about: We often suffer. In fact, what Habakkuk describes is financial and social ruin. Looking ahead to the Israelites' captivity in Babylon, Habakkuk knew he'd be caught in a boiling cauldron of pain. But notice what Habakkuk says about the pain to come: "Though the fig tree does not bud and there are no grapes on the vine"—in other words, no matter what happens—"*yet* I will rejoice in the LORD." It's that "yet" which points toward the real faith lesson in this book. The prophet was willing to trust in God, rely on Him, and place his confidence in God's actions regardless of the circumstance.

Habakkuk doesn't command believers from all generations to pretend as if their pain doesn't really hurt. Neither does he encourage resignation, stoicism, or some mistaken smile-at-all-costs mentality. He *does* encourage joy. He contends that even when our sovereign Lord allows suffering and loss, our joy need not wane.

Notice where we find our joy. "I will rejoice in the LORD. I will be joyful in *God my Savior.*" Habakkuk declares that, even in the midst of pain, we can sustain a deep inner sense of peace and joy because of God's goodness. Life is hard, but God is good.

I imagine Habakkuk came to this realization one day while standing on a mountain trail. Out of the corner of his eye, he saw movement: a deer, sure-footed even though it was walking the heights of a peak. At that moment, Habakkuk saw a physical representation of his faith walk. God was asking Habakkuk to walk on the heights, too. The prophet would have to live a step from destruction as his nation fell in ruins around him. Despite this foreboding, Habakkuk had hope: "He makes my feet like the feet of a deer, he enables me to go on the heights."

One day—maybe even today—you'll face difficulty. When that happens, you can choose to rejoice in God and place your trust in Him. If you do, you'll experience His divine enabling. You'll "go on the heights." When you encounter that difficult time in your life, remember this: Life is hard, but God is good.

REFLECTIONS: Is there some "fig tree" that isn't "budding" for you right now? What can you do to gain God's perspective and receive from Him the ability to endure?

PRAYER FOCUS: Spend a few moments receiving God's power and experiencing the joy of His presence. Ask Him to enable you to endure the trials you face.

96
WHEN YOUR SHIP IS SINKING

Without warning, a furious storm came up on the lake, so that the
waves swept over the boat. But Jesus was sleeping. The disciples went
and woke him, saying, "Lord, save us! We're going to drown!"
He replied, "You of little faith, why are you so afraid?" Then
he got up and rebuked the winds and the waves,
and it was completely calm.

MATTHEW 8:24–26

Are you dealing with a crisis? Are relational or financial storms beating down on you? If so, you just might find some encouragement from this moment in Jesus' life.

Storms are inevitable. That's simply the way life operates. Sometimes people wonder if they're out of God's will because a trial or crisis rages in their lives. Before you beat yourself up, pause to consider that you may be exactly where God wants you. After all, in this story the disciples had followed Jesus right into that little boat; in His presence, the storm hit. You may be following Jesus right now and just experiencing the inevitable storms of life.

Storms can hit so suddenly. The storm in Matthew 8:24–26 hit "without warning." In the same way, you won't always have advance notice when a crisis intrudes into your life. One moment life may be bright, and the next, dark clouds may blot out the sun.

Remember, too, that storms are impartial. No one receives special exemption from life's pain. All of us experience our share. As a pastor, I can tell you that at one time or another, most families face crises such as an unexpected death, a rebellious child, or lost employment.

Since storms are inevitable in life, believers face just one question regarding them: "How will I respond to this storm?"

According to Matthew's story, we can respond to the storms of life in one of two ways: with fear or with faith.

Fear, of course, comes naturally. When your ship is sinking, panic rises, and soon all you see is the storm itself and its destructive potential. For example, when an unexpected expense arises and you don't have money to pay it, fear may come flooding into your life. In such a situation, it's quite easy to let healthy concern turn into unhealthy anxiety. Soon your thinking is dominated by thoughts of possible disaster: *Oh, no, what's going to happen? How will this all work out?*

The alternative to fear is faith. At its core, faith is simply trust in God. It's a convinced awareness, not only of what He *can* do but of what He *will* do. Faith in the middle of a storm means confessing your dependence upon God. It means praying, understanding that your Father will act with your best interests at heart. It means resting in Him, knowing that He has heard and will answer your requests.

When the waves start to rock your boat, when your ship is sinking, remember that *Jesus is in the boat with you.* No matter how rough the waters become, He'll see you through.

REFLECTIONS: Are you enduring a crisis right now? How can you respond in faith? If you're not experiencing a difficulty at present, how can you prepare yourself to respond in faith to the next one that comes along?

PRAYER FOCUS: Confess your dependence upon God. If you're experiencing a crisis today, ask the Lord to help. If you're not, ask Him to strengthen your faith for any difficulties you may face in the future.

97
THE POWER OF
ONE VOICE

*"For if you remain silent at this time, relief and deliverance for the
Jews will arise from another place, but you and your father's
family will perish. And who knows but that you have
come to royal position for such a time as this?"*

ESTHER 4:14

Spouses depend upon each other daily, and rightly so. Such inter-
dependence is healthy. But times will arise when one of you will
have to act alone. For one reason or another, your partner won't be
able to help you. The responsibility will fall squarely, and solely, on
your shoulders. At those times, you'll want to remember how one
person can make a difference.

Many centuries ago, Queen Esther received a divine reminder
of the power of one. God presented Esther, the Jewish wife of King
Xerxes, with a chance to make a difference. King Xerxes had
decreed that all Jews had to die, not knowing that Esther herself
was Jewish. Her uncle, Mordecai, understood that she alone had
access to the king's ear. Mordecai's desperate plea caught her attention: "Who knows but that you have come to royal position for such
a time as this?"

That was all she needed to hear. Risking her life, she gained an
audience with the king and said what she needed to say. Through
her, God saved the entire nation of Israel.

The Bible is full of such stories, instances when God used one
person for a specific task that made all the difference. Daniel
revealed the one true God to Nebuchadnezzar, King of Babylon
(Daniel 2:27–28). Joseph rose to power in Egypt and saved Israel
from starvation (Genesis 50:20). God chose Gideon to save Israel
from Midian (Judges 6:14). The list goes on and on—Rahab, Ruth,

Peter, Paul—century after century. Each person had to take responsibility and act alone to accomplish God's will.

People feel small, insignificant, powerless these days. They wonder if their solitary actions can really accomplish anything meaningful. I believe God brings each one of us into positions in which our particular voices are needed. Jobs, schools, churches, families, and communities all present opportunities for personal involvement that will make a positive difference.

Suppose your company is about to make a mistake. The higher-ups are contemplating taking on more debt than the company can handle. You know you have to say something. Your marriage partner can't walk into that boardroom with you. You, and you alone, are responsible for acting. *Yours* is the voice the company needs to hear.

Suppose one of your friends accepts Christ and you're the logical one to disciple her. Your choice to act, to take responsibility, will make a big difference in that person's life. While your spouse can encourage you, *you'll* be the one to actually roll up your sleeves and do the work.

Sometimes a task doesn't call for you and your spouse, you and a friend, you and a coworker, or you and a committee. It calls for you, and you alone, to stand up, make the call, and go for it. Such a call may involve sacrifice. It may involve risk. But who knows whether God Himself will not have brought you to that position for a specific reason?

Don't underestimate what God can do through the power of one...through *you!*

REFLECTIONS: In what way does God want you to take personal responsibility right now? To what position has God brought you so that you can make a difference?

PRAYER FOCUS: Pray for discernment in the weeks ahead about where God wants to use you. Then pray for courage to take responsibility when the time is right.

98
IN PRAISE OF MOTHERS

A wife of noble character who can find? She is worth far more than rubies.... Her children arise and call her blessed.

PROVERBS 31:10, 28

Feeling a little beat up lately, Mom? Wondering if all your efforts really amount to anything in your children's lives? Then read on, and be encouraged.

For years, I've invited church newcomers to a getting-to-know-you gathering at my home. One of the questions I usually ask at this event is "When you were seven to twelve years old, who or what was the center of warmth in your life?" Do you want to know the number one answer I've received over the years? Perhaps you won't be surprised to learn that most people have said, "My mother."

Sometimes moms read Proverbs 31 and feel overwhelmed. "How can I measure up?" they cry. Or, "I work outside the home. I don't have time to be a Proverbs 31 woman!" But the key thought in this passage is in verse 10: "A wife of noble character who can find?" It's noble character that makes all the difference in a mom. Everyone has strengths and weaknesses, but moms who develop and exhibit character give their children an inexpressibly valuable gift. Your life, your character, your example will speak to your children in a thousand different ways.

My mom knew what it meant to work hard. Her parents were sharecroppers in Texas; she learned how to pick cotton early in life. She couldn't finish high school because her parents needed her to work. She married at the tender age of eighteen, raised five children, and held down a full-time job. Most of the time, she was happy and cheerful. She rarely complained, was full of fun, and made sure her children felt loved. Was she perfect? No way! But she gave to her children in a self-sacrificing way that, looking back, seems truly amazing. What character!

My wife's mom is perhaps the most generous person I know. For years she gathered secondhand items of all kinds—clothes, cribs, infant car seats—and literally showered new moms with gifts. She worked full time at the University of Washington's library, was a mother, and taught Sunday school. Instead of complaining about her workload, she always had something positive to say about her husband, her day, her church, and her life. What character!

My wife is a great mother to our children. Naomi usually thinks of our family before herself. She is unfailingly kind to us all. She exhibits patience in almost every situation, including spilt milk, forgotten chores, and lost homework. Her unconditional love floods our home with warmth and joy. Our children feel that love in significant ways every day. What character!

Mom, regardless of your job, talents, looks, bank account, or parenting style, you can be a mother of "noble character" and have a tremendous impact upon your children's lives. In fact, you're probably doing so right now, more than you know.

So be encouraged. As you pursue noble character, remember that you're worth far more than rubies. And someday, your children will arise and call you blessed.

REFLECTIONS: Wives, share with your husbands how you feel about your mothering. Husbands, use this time to affirm your wives' character and mothering skills.

PRAYER FOCUS: Ask God to build noble character within you. Ask Him to provide wisdom, strength, and perseverance as you parent your children.

99
IN PRAISE OF FATHERS

Solomon answered, "You have shown great kindness to your
servant, my father David, because he was faithful to you
and righteous and upright in heart."

1 KINGS 3:6

Being a father is one of the toughest jobs in the world. Success in business is a breeze compared to the rigors of successful fathering. If the truth were told, many fathers feel inadequate in this role, even though they do the best they can. And frankly, our society can come down pretty hard on fathers. People tend to think about all the ways fathers fail rather than all the ways they succeed.

Let's slide into our desk chairs and take a lesson from Solomon concerning fatherhood. When Solomon was about twenty years old, he stood before God as king. In a conversation with Him, Solomon talked about his own father. What did he remember about David? I'm sure he remembered many things, but what he mentioned first is this: "He was faithful to you and righteous and upright in heart." How's that for a good report? "My father, David, had integrity. He was a man of faith who served You." Solomon remembered positive traits that affected how his father lived his life.

But wait a minute. How could Solomon say this? Think about all of David's failures. We know about David's adultery with Bathsheba and the tragic murder that accompanied the attempted coverup. We remember that David allowed his son Amnon to commit a vicious crime against Tamar without consequence. We know that he took a census of Israel against God's wishes.

That's all true. David made mistakes as a man and as a father, but in spite of his failures, his son Solomon remembered positive traits such as faithfulness, righteousness, and being upright in heart. With character like that, the good things David did far outweighed the bad.

I'm not implying that fathers should shrug their shoulders and say, "That's the way I am" or ignore the deficiencies in their lives. I do think, however, that dads should cut themselves some slack.

Take Solomon's lesson and apply it. Think about your life, your character. Do you love God? Do you place Him first in your life? Have you sometimes had to stand alone, holding out for what was right, even though it was unpopular? Have you put your arms around your family, protecting and caring for them even when it cost you? Have you gently taught your children what it means to follow God? Have you beaten back pride and admitted your mistakes? Have you coupled your parenting standards with God's grace as you've disciplined your children?

Nobody knows your imperfections as a father better than you do, but chances are, your answers to these questions indicate that you're a man of character. When your kids remember you, they'll more than likely say, "He was faithful to God and righteous and upright in heart." Since that's true, the positive things you say and do far outweigh your deficiencies.

Next time you're feeling inadequate, think of Solomon's assessment of his father. Remember that a father who follows God, even though he makes mistakes, will positively impact his family.

REFLECTIONS: Husbands, share with your wives how you feel about your fathering. Wives, use this time to affirm your husbands' character and fathering skills.

PRAYER FOCUS: Thank God for the good things you see in your partner's parenting. Together, ask God to enable you to parent your children well.

100
CONTENTMENT
FOR TODAY

*But godliness with contentment is great gain. For we brought nothing
into the world, and we can take nothing out of it. But if we have
food and clothing, we will be content with that.*

1 TIMOTHY 6:6–8

Contentment. It seems to be one commodity lacking in today's
world. Late-night television abounds with hour-long infomercials
telling us that we can succeed in real estate and live in the lap of luxury. The implication? That *then* we'll be content.

Of course, these commercials only tap our human dissatisfaction with the status quo. Instead of being satisfied with what we
have, we tend to want *more*. This is a trap that eventually can leave
us overextended, disillusioned, and above all, dissatisfied.

"But the Bible exhorts us to work hard," someone might
respond. Absolutely. Hard work is positive. "What's wrong with
ambition?" another asks. Not a thing. Paul himself was a man who
approached his calling with passion. "Well, then, what's the deal?"

The deal is this: Contentment is for today, not tomorrow. We
can so easily get caught in "if/then" thinking. *If* I snag that promotion, *then* I'll be happy. *If* I buy a new house, *then* I'll be content. But
contentment on the installment plan never works. The "then"
never materializes because there's always a new "if."

You know how fleeting happiness can be. It's a subjective emotional state based upon current circumstances. If "happy" things
take place, then you experience "happiness." Contentment, on the
other hand, is a deep inner sense of joy, independent of circumstances, drawn from the inexhaustible wells of God's goodness.
This joy is based on God's good gifts that often don't increase our
bank balances or our belongings: friendships, family, service, and

especially a close relationship with Him.

Paul said it clearly: "Godliness with contentment is great gain." Hunt's paraphrase: "When contentment accompanies my relationship with God, regardless of my financial status, I've really hit the jackpot."

Each of us must foster an attitude that moves us in this direction. And make no mistake about it, contentment *is* a state of mind. Paul himself, the writer of almost half of the New Testament, said, "I have *learned* to be content" (Philippians 4:11). Paul *learned* to fight the lie that equates happiness with status, money, or power. He *learned* to tell himself the truth when thoughts of "poor me" crept into his mind. You and I can do the same.

Don't let the prospects of tomorrow rob you of contentment today. Take joy in what you do, who you are, and in what God has given you. Be content with the basics. You'll find that you enjoy life so much more without that little background voice constantly telling you that you aren't what you *could* be or that you don't have what you *could* have.

Want to hit the jackpot? Look inside, and find the sense of contentment and joy that God wants to give you.

REFLECTIONS: Are you a contented person? Are you learning contentment as a couple? If not, how can you foster a contented attitude in yourselves?

PRAYER FOCUS: Ask God for His perspective on contentment and for a renewed sense of joy for this day and the days to come.

101
FILLING YOUR CHILDREN'S EMOTIONAL TANKS

Fathers, do not embitter your children,
or they will become discouraged.
COLOSSIANS 3:21

Want to avoid embittering your kids? to ensure that your children don't become discouraged? Then actively choose to fill your children's "emotional tanks" every day.

What's an emotional tank? I first heard of this concept from Christian psychiatrist Ross Campbell. Campbell uses the phrase to symbolize a child's subjective sense of feeling loved. When a child receives a clear message from her parents that she is loved, a deep emotional need is met in her life. At that moment, a child's emotional tank is "full." And a full emotional tank usually means that a child will be happy, healthy, and able to do her best in life.

As parents, we have the responsibility of expressing love to our children in ways they understand, keeping their tanks full each day. In other words, wise parents proactively and effectively *transmit* love to their children. They communicate love in tangible ways that their children comprehend.

Three specific behaviors can help ensure that your message of love comes through loud and clear. First, give your children *affection.* Hugs, kisses, holding hands, pats on the back, shoulder rubs—all help your young ones feel loved. In fact, no matter what age your children are, physical touch demonstrates love in a tangible way that your kids can understand.

You can also express love through *affirmation,* an expression of your children's value. This certainly happens when you say encouraging words that convey what your children mean to you. But speaking positive words isn't the only way to affirm your kids. Ross

Campbell suggests another method of affirmation that makes a big difference: positive eye contact. To convey unconditional love to your children, give them positive eye contact throughout the day. Without realizing it, parents often use eye contact to convey anger or irritation. Instead, make it a practice to express love by looking directly at your children and smiling.

Finally, express love to your children through *attention*. This is probably the number-one way kids sense your love. Of course, you can spend time with your entire family during dinner, games, and prayer at the end of the day. These times feed everyone's need for attention. But also seek to spend time with each child individually. It's one of the best ways to fill each child's emotional tank. Do you know that spending ten minutes playing with your preschooler can fill his tank for hours? That an hour with your daughter on a "date" at McDonald's will encourage her for weeks to come?

Make sure your little ones don't become discouraged, that they don't spend their days embittered. Consciously do things to help fill their emotional tanks every day.

REFLECTIONS: How are you doing at keeping your children's emotional tanks full? What are you doing well? What could you do better?

PRAYER FOCUS: Ask God to help you be aware of ways to help your children feel loved. Invite Him to show you apt times for expressing affection, affirmation, and attention.

102
FUN AROUND
THE DINNER TABLE

A cheerful look brings joy to the heart,
and good news gives health to the bones.
PROVERBS 15:30

Maybe it's my warped personality, but I can't imagine family life without a lot of laughter. I want to laugh with my family, to share fun with the ones I love. The smiles, the giggles, the unsuppressed guffaws of family life somehow deepen the connection among us all. I'm sure you've felt it in your family, too—the kinship of shared laughter.

Applied to families, Proverbs 15:30 couldn't be plainer: The cheerful interactions of a happy family will infuse each and every heart with joy and health.

Spontaneous laughter happens in all the nooks and crannies of Hunt family life, but one place is a perfect forum for such fun—the dinner table. Ostensibly we're there to eat, but I always have another agenda for our mealtimes. I'm there to connect with my family: to talk, to laugh, to love. It's the family oasis at the end of the day's activities, bringing refreshment on a number of levels.

There's usually a lot of laughter around our dinner table, and there's nothing I like better. That unintended slip of the tongue, that witty rejoinder, or just the fun of trying to make sense of the day's activities often yields rich veins of golden laughter. We make our own fun together, and our hearts are the better for it.

My family was having dinner together recently, and after we had eaten, we sat around the table and talked. Soon we were think-ing about dessert. As it so happened, my oldest daughter, Jenny, had made brownies the day before. But as she mixed the batter, this straight-A high-school student had inadvertently left out a major ingredient: sugar! The brownies tasted somewhere between dog biscuits and stale bread, but we hadn't gotten around to throwing them away.

As we considered our options for dessert that night, Jenny grinned mischievously and said, "Hey, how about my brownies?"

Poking fun, I said, "All right everyone, let's all point our fingers at Jenny to punish her for the terrible brownies." We all pointed at Jenny, laughing together at our silliness. Amused, Jenny stuck out her tongue at us.

That's when my son Jon said, "Those brownies are so bad; let's take them outside and burn them."

"Good idea," I said, grabbing the pan of brownies. "Everybody follow me." We opened the sliding-glass door and marched into the backyard chanting, "Bad brownies, bad brownies, bad brownies." We threw the brownies into an old flowerpot and had a mock burning. Back inside, we all laughed together at our dinner nonsense.

I'll tell you something about those few minutes. Our time together that night brought laughter to our faces and joy to our hearts. While our fun is usually not as silly, our shared laughter always lightens our hearts and brings us closer together.

Of course, every family is different. There are no prescriptions when it comes to a sense of humor, but still, do you have fun together? Does laughter erupt around your dinner table from time to time? When you look back on your times with your family, your opportunities to laugh together will be among your most memorable moments.

REFLECTIONS: When was the last time your family enjoyed a good laugh together? What can you do to make your family times, including your evening meal, even more enjoyable?
PRAYER FOCUS: Pray for the gift of laughter in your home and for God's joy to touch your hearts.

103
SECOND THOUGHTS

Jesus replied, "No one who puts his hand to the plow and looks back is fit for service in the kingdom of God."

LUKE 9:62

Second thoughts—you've probably had them from time to time. You remember a decision you made in the past, maybe years ago, and wonder if you chose correctly. You wonder, *Did I go to the right college?* or *Did I take the right career path?* or *Did I let the Lord down when I didn't go into full-time ministry?* You might even feel a twinge of guilt over a decision you made long ago.

In Luke 9:62, Jesus clearly states that His children shouldn't play this game. He releases us from the jagged pain of looking back. You might say, "But you don't understand. I resisted God's will." Actually, I do understand. But do you think you're the first of God's children to resist Him? How about Abraham, Moses, Jonah, Peter, and a host of others? Didn't God still accomplish wonderful things through each one of them? Yes! If you've resisted God, you do need His forgiveness, but after He has graciously forgiven you, don't second-guess yourself.

Perhaps your situation wasn't a matter of disobedience. Maybe you did the best you could to obey God. You wanted to do His will. And yet, years later, you have second thoughts about your decision, and you're beating yourself up. You wonder, *Did I miss God's best? Is His perfect will still possible for me?*

Once again, Jesus' analogy in Luke 9:62 helps us understand the destructive nature of second thoughts. Envision a person leaning into a plow, churning up the dirt of a fertile field. But instead of straight rows, the worker has created uneven zigzags of plowed earth. The reason is obvious: Instead of keeping his eyes on his task, the worker constantly looked over his shoulder.

Second thoughts about yesterday won't help you a bit with today. In fact, looking back only serves to ruin what God wants you to do in the here and now.

Paul Stevens helps us understand how God works with mistakes in our lives, whether intentional or unintentional. Maybe this analogy will help you avoid looking back:

> I love the way Persian rugs are made. Two long poles are erected on which the body of the rug is stretched. On one side is the master rug-maker who, knowing the overall intended design, calls out the color and position of the threads for the weavers standing on the opposite side to insert. Inevitably there are errors in communication and understanding. The designer, seeing an obvious error from his side that is not apparent to the weavers, makes allowances by redesigning the overall plan. His purpose is more important than his detailed plan. Our God can make something beautiful out of our lives no matter what we have done. Otherwise the gospel is good news only for the flawless.[1]

Stevens has it right: God, the master designer, is more than capable of incorporating any "weaving error" into His overall plan. He can take our mistakes and make "something beautiful out of our lives no matter what we have done."

So don't allow second thoughts to immobilize you. Don't let regrets about the past ruin today. Let them go, and let God continue to weave His plan in your life.

REFLECTIONS: Have second thoughts plagued you recently? Are you ready to let them go?

PRAYER FOCUS: Spend a few moments releasing the past—especially those second thoughts—to God. Then take a moment to dedicate the present and future to Him.

104
"I NEED YOU"

Two are better than one... If one falls down,
his friend can help him up.
ECCLESIASTES 4:9–10

Self-sufficiency. Most of us admire this quality, but it has one draw-back. Without intending to, you can push your partner away with your attempts at self-sufficiency. In effect, they communicate the message "I don't need you."

Listen to what Christian psychologist Alan Loy McGinnis says about this issue:

> So the cardinal rule for developing intimacy: Dare to be needy. The person who shows vulnerable sides to us and says "I need you" is hard to resist.
>
> "Do you know when I felt closest to my husband?" asked a pert and black-eyed wife. "It was when I found out that he was terrified of bears!" Her husband is a husky and self-confident airline pilot, and she hadn't known he was afraid of anything, but when he became more vulnerable he became more lovable.[1]

Think about that last statement: "When he became more vul-nerable he became more lovable." Vulnerability is the central issue. When you become more transparent with each other about your fears, faults, failures, and needs, you communicate trust in each other. You open the door to the inner you. Not only will you draw closer to each other, you'll receive the help that Ecclesiastes 4:10 describes: "If one falls down, his friend can help him up."

Now, I'm not talking about being a weakling or drumming up some fake fear to share. Rather, I want to encourage you to be

226

genuine in your weakness. You know what it feels like when your spouse needs you; he wants to feel that sensation, too. Learn to speak a need when you feel it, and you'll open the door to each other's heart.

I don't want to sound sexist, but generally speaking, men find this difficult. Many men think they must be strong at all costs. But there's a difference between being strong and being hard. A strong man communicates a need when he has one, inviting his wife into his world and gaining her support. A hard man remains stoic at all costs, hiding his deepest needs and distancing himself emotionally from his wife.

So how do you learn to express your weakness? Start by sharing your feelings. Often, when we're afraid to admit our needs, we communicate facts or opinions rather than feelings. Facts, while important to communicate, keep your partner at the surface: "I had a talk with my boss today." Opinions go a bit deeper—"My boss made an unreasonable request of me"—but they still don't invite your spouse completely into your heart. Feelings, however, begin to express need: "After my discussion with my boss today, I'm feeling overwhelmed. He wants me to take on a whole new area of responsibility." Do you see the difference? Sharing your feelings communicates the message "I trust you, and I need your support."

Your partner wants you to reveal yourself. He wants to be needed, and he has something to offer you. Are you ready and willing to reveal your needs and let your spouse into your world?

REFLECTIONS: Do your words and actions communicate "I need you" to each other? Do you share your feelings, even your feelings of fear or depression? Why or why not? What can you do to encourage each other to be vulnerable?

PRAYER FOCUS: Share prayer requests with each other. Be vulnerable as you share. Then spend time praying for the needs that you both mention.

105
THE NEHEMIAH
PRINCIPLE

But when Sanballat, Tobiah, the Arabs, the Ammonites and the men
of Ashdod heard that the repairs to Jerusalem's walls had gone ahead
and that the gaps were being closed, they were very angry. They
all plotted together to come and fight against Jerusalem and
stir up trouble against it. But we prayed to our God and
posted a guard day and night to meet this threat.

NEHEMIAH 4:7–9

Life is full of challenges. I'd guess that if you looked back over your marriage, you'd remember a few times when things looked a little dicey, times you wondered how things would turn out. But somehow you made it through.

And someday, maybe even today, you'll have new challenges to overcome. How will you make it through yet again?

Nehemiah has something to say to believers facing challenges. Nehemiah was an Old Testament Jewish leader who left his comfortable position in Persia to rebuild the walls around Jerusalem. That project tested the limits of his courage and abilities. In fact, he faced a series of challenges that threatened the completion of the project, but with God's help, he overcame each one.

How did he do it? Several factors were involved, but the verses above outline the most important one. I call it the "Nehemiah Principle." The last verse demonstrates how Nehemiah overcame each challenge: "But we prayed to our God and posted a guard day and night to meet this threat."

The Nehemiah Principle says two things: Do everything you *can* do, and ask God to do everything you *can't*.

A plot was brewing against Nehemiah that could have delayed the project and even resulted in loss of life. When Nehemiah learned of the plot, his first response was prayer. It was just that simple. He took his concerns to God, knowing that his ultimate success depended upon God's intervention. But Nehemiah didn't stop there. He also "posted a guard day and night" to meet the threat. Nehemiah didn't cop out on his responsibility. God would do everything Nehemiah *couldn't* do, but there were plenty of ways Nehemiah *could* be involved.

We often have the tendency, I think, to do one or the other as we face life's challenges. Either we pray and neglect positive ways to intervene ourselves, or we forge ahead, forgetting to invite God into difficult situations. The best resolution to a challenge emerges when we do both.

I recently talked with parents whose elementary-age son was showing signs of rebellion. He wasn't responding to his school-teacher's authority, and he was becoming harder to handle at home. Children often present challenges of one kind or another to their parents, and this particular one is not uncommon.

Together, we devised a plan to handle this challenge. First, these parents would pray together daily for their young son. They would ask God to soften their son's heart. They would ask God to give wisdom to each person who might have influence in their son's life. In other words, they asked God to do things they couldn't.

In addition to prayer, these parents needed to do some things themselves to meet the challenge they faced. This included becoming more consistent in their discipline and spending more time with their son. They found success as they "prayed to [their] God and posted a guard day and night to meet this threat."

What challenges do you face today? Whatever they are, do everything you *can* do, and ask God to do everything you *can't*.

REFLECTIONS: Do you need to apply the Nehemiah Principle to a challenge you face today? How might you put it into practice in the days to come?

PRAYER FOCUS: Pray specifically for that challenge in your life. Ask God to do what you can't and for wisdom and courage to do what you can.

106
GOD'S CALL

"Ah, Sovereign LORD," I said, "I do not know how to speak; I am only a child." But the LORD said to me, "Do not say, 'I am only a child.' You must go to everyone I send you to and say whatever I command you. Do not be afraid of them, for I am with you."

JEREMIAH 1:6–8

Have you ever had an argument with God about His will for your life?

Jeremiah did. Before Jeremiah was even born, God had a plan for him. God had appointed him as a prophet to the nations. When the right time came, God showed Jeremiah what He wanted him to do. And when Jeremiah responded, he did so with a typical human reaction, immediately offering reasons he *couldn't* respond to God's call. "There, that settles it. I'm young and inexperienced," Jeremiah said, "so I just won't be able to do what God wants me to do."

We so quickly disqualify ourselves from God's service, don't we? I'm too young; I'm too old; I'm not good enough; I don't have the time; I lack the skill; I don't have what it takes. We look at our weaknesses and plead our insufficiency before God.

When I was twenty-two years old and a first-year schoolteacher, my pastor asked me to lead a home Bible study. I had never done anything like that before. My first thought was *I can't do this; I don't know enough.*

But our inadequacies are never the most important factor when God has a purpose for us. Jeremiah 1:6–8 illustrates the fact that when God calls us to be or do something, *He* equips us for the task and sustains us in the process. Think about Jesus calling His first disciples. Peter dropped to his knees and said, "Go away from me, Lord; I am a sinful man!" (Luke 5:8). He pleaded his inadequacy and inability to fulfill the call. But eventually, Peter focused not on what he lacked but on what Christ would provide. Like Jeremiah before him, Peter had to rely on God's promise: "Do not be afraid of them, for I am with you." It's His presence in our lives that qualifies us for His calling—His sufficiency, not ours.

Think about your own lives for a moment. You know that God's plan for you includes ministry to others. Maybe He wants you to teach a Sunday-school class or volunteer at a local food bank. Perhaps you feel God's leading to go on a short-term mission or simply befriend someone who seems lonely. Or maybe He's calling you to make a dramatic change that will significantly impact your lives.

When you first think about this call, you'll probably feel inadequate. You'll immediately think of at least one good reason you can't do it. If nothing else, you'll say with Peter, "I am a sinful man."

My advice? Don't argue with God. Accept His call; He knows what He's doing. With Jeremiah, learn that if God calls you, He will certainly equip and sustain you.

REFLECTIONS: Have you been avoiding a call, large or small, because you feel inadequate to fulfill it? What can you do to respond in faith, knowing that God will work through you?

PRAYER FOCUS: Pray for an increased awareness of God's ability to equip and sustain you for whatever He wants you to do. Ask Him to help you say yes whenever He calls.

107
SHARING YOUR LIFE

The man and his wife were both naked,
and they felt no shame.
GENESIS 2:25

Do you share your feelings with each other? Do you reveal your inner worlds to each other?

Genesis 2:25 depicts a relationship without shame, a marriage with no barriers to true vulnerability. This verse illustrates what a marital relationship should be, and people today indicate a desire to share their deepest selves in this way. In a recent secular poll, husbands and wives agreed that "the ability to talk to each other about feelings" was one of the most important components of a good marriage.[1]

However, this skill does not come easy, especially for men. Dr. James Dobson, author and psychologist, has said that "the inability or unwillingness of husbands to reveal their feelings to their wives is one of the common complaints of women."[2] One husband, interested in improving his skills in this area, recently made a statement to me which is typical of men: "My capacity to express my feelings seems so crude and halting—it doesn't even come close to my wife's skill in this area. When Connie asks me how I feel, I just don't know what to say."

For husbands *and* wives, *recognizing what's going on inside* is the first step in sharing. Often spouses have difficulties sharing with each other because they don't know what they're feeling themselves. Instead of spending time examining what's going on inside, some people tend to intellectualize or simply ignore their emotions. If this is true of you, try to make a habit of examining your heart. Are you sad or angry? Are you scared or disappointed? Are you happy or excited? Pause for a moment and ask yourself, *If I could put this feeling into words, what would they be?*

Recognizing your emotions is the first step. *Actually sharing such feelings* is the next. When you've become aware of your feelings, there are two steps to communicating them. First, share the context for your feelings, that is, the events or situations that led to your feelings. For example, "I'm very tired tonight" or "Today one of the people I work with complimented me" or "We haven't had much time together recently." Then, after you explain the context, simply share the emotions you feel.

Listen to this wife's words to her husband: "The baby is teething again and has been so fussy all day. I feel like I'm losing my ability to cope." A simple bit of information, but so vital to the marriage relationship. Whenever you share these kinds of statements, you let your spouse into your world.

The third step is simply to *provide a safe environment when your partner shares, offering understanding and acceptance.* If your partner decides to be vulnerable with you, she will be watching for your response. If you give her understanding and acceptance, she'll lower more barriers and share on deeper and deeper levels. As a couple, you'll make progress in sharing thoughts, ideas, and emotions only if you both feel safe.

Go ahead. Bring down the walls. Share your worlds. And enjoy the intimacy that such sharing will bring.

REFLECTIONS: Are you able to share your deepest selves with each other? If so, affirm the aspects of your relationship that encourage this sharing. If not, try to figure out why not. Do you need to work on one of the three steps mentioned above?

PRAYER FOCUS: Ask for God's help in being vulnerable with each other and in expressing acceptance during your times of sharing.

108
WHEN ACCEPTANCE
IS HARD

But the fruit of the Spirit is love....patience, kindness.
GALATIANS 5:22

No matter how close you are as a couple, you'll inevitably encounter aspects of each other that will drive you up the wall. (Perhaps you can name such a trait in each other at this very moment!)

For example, maybe one of you has a high tolerance for belongings strewn through the house—on couches, tables, chairs, and other highly visible places. Or maybe one of you, no matter how early you set that alarm, just can't make it anywhere on time. Often these traits persist, failing to change year after year. Discussion helps for just a little while. You devise action plans only to have them eventually lapse into disuse. Then the behavior reappears like a nagging pest.

You know you should accept each other regardless of your weaknesses, but living with an imperfect partner isn't easy. What does "accepting your partner" mean, anyway? As you work to accept each other, what practical steps should you take? Do you have to smile and pretend that you enjoy arriving at church thirty minutes late? Are you required to laugh when you find your kitchen dismantled?

While God doesn't say we must enjoy our partner's shortcomings, He does encourage us to face them with love, patience, and kindness. True acceptance happens only in the context of such godly attitudes. As Christians, we simply don't have the option to give the cold shoulder, withhold kindness, or punish each other.

What makes this so difficult is that when your spouse does something unpleasant, you'll definitely feel the sting of disappointment. Accepting your spouse doesn't mean that you feel happy when he does something you don't like. However, it does mean that you'll go beyond your feelings of displeasure and choose to accept your spouse, to be patient and express kindness despite your disappointment.

Of course, you can't make such a choice without a second and vital part of acceptance: forgiveness. You can't, after all, accept a partner whom you resent. To the degree that you can release ongoing forgiveness for your partner's weaknesses or blind spots, you'll also be able to grant true acceptance.

Genuine acceptance, then, involves both patience *and* forgiveness. My friend Dennis is a perfect example of this. His wife, Jane, is habitually late. When they were first married, Dennis's blood pressure soared as time and again they were late because of Jane. Now, twenty years later, I observe loving acceptance. Dennis knows that Jane won't change. This trait is too much a part of her character. Instead of punishing her, however, he has accepted her. He chooses love, patience, and kindness. When necessary, he forgives her. And he has figured out ways to meet his own needs. For example, he takes his own vehicle if he wants to be sure to arrive on time. But when Jane does make them late, he chooses to accept her. (By the way, acceptance goes both ways. Dennis has a trait or two that Jane has had to accept as well!)

You may be feeling the brunt of each other's irritating habits or enduring blind spots this week. Let me encourage you to demonstrate genuine acceptance. It's one of the best choices you'll ever make to build your marriage.

REFLECTIONS: Do you both feel accepted by each other? Have you forgiven each other for your blind spots? Do you need to take some steps to help each other feel accepted despite your shortcomings?
PRAYER FOCUS: Pray for a fresh infusion of God's love, patience, and kindness toward each other. Ask for the ability to express acceptance to each other on a daily basis.

109
STRENGTH WHEN
YOU NEED IT

David was greatly distressed because the men were talking of stoning
him; each one was bitter in spirit because of his sons and daughters.
But David found strength in the LORD his God.

1 SAMUEL 30:6

Are you at the end of your rope? Do things looking decidedly
bleak?

You're in good company. David found himself "greatly distressed" when he and his men returned home to find that the
Amalekites had taken their wives and children captive. Not only
had David's own family been taken, but his men were seriously
considering stoning him because of their bitter losses. This was definitely one of the low spots of David's life. Can you imagine David's
state of mind as he stared into space, shocked and shattered? What
could he do? How could he rectify the situation?

I've always been fascinated by David's solution to the problem.
Contained within the last eight words of 1 Samuel 30:6 is a principle
that helped David in his time of need...and it can help believers
today. The principle is simple: When you are distressed, find
strength in the Lord your God.

I have news for you. If you try to do anything worthwhile in
life, you'll encounter difficulty and sometimes discouragement.
Check the biographies of Christians past and present, and one
thing becomes clear: People such as Billy Graham, James Dobson,
and Chuck Colson didn't succeed without experiencing major dis-
appointments, times in their lives when they were "greatly
distressed." At such times, these men did what David did; they
found strength in the Lord.

God makes it clear that He wants to help you along life's roller coaster ride. "For the eyes of the LORD," Scripture says, "range throughout the earth to strengthen those whose hearts are fully committed to him" (2 Chronicles 16:9). When you go to God, you'll find the strength you need.

What practical steps can you take to strengthen yourself in God? First Samuel 30:6 doesn't give specifics, but I'll tell you two things that probably happened. First, David went to God and poured out his heart. All you have to do is read the Psalms of David to understand his conversations with God. He didn't hesitate to bring his troubles to the Lord and say what was on his mind.

David not only laid bare before the Lord everything in his mind and heart, he also spent enough time with God to gain His perspective and direction. In the book of Psalms, David expresses again and again how he remembers God's truth through prayer. Psalm 23, for example, expresses God's perspective on His relationship with us. And when you gain His perspective, you can't help but be encouraged and filled with hope.

When you feel encouraged, you'll also be free to act. Instead of passively waiting for the worst, you'll look for direction and move ahead. David certainly did. After finding strength in the Lord, he immediately asked God what to do and did what God told him. He pursued his attackers and brought every single person and belonging back home. He left nothing behind.

Want to find strength in the Lord? Run to Him when you're distressed, and tell Him what's happening in your life. Gain His perspective, and find encouragement and direction when you need them most.

REFLECTIONS: What difficulties have caused or are causing you "great distress"? Are you finding strength in the Lord?
PRAYER FOCUS: Go to the Lord in your distress, and pour out your heart. Then pause and listen for His perspective and direction.

110
THE BALANCE OF MUTUAL ACCOUNTABILITY

*You, my brothers, were called to be free. But do not use your freedom
to indulge the sinful nature; rather, serve one another in love.*

GALATIANS 5:13

Have you encountered the balancing act of freedom versus
accountability in your marriage? You have something you want to
do, and you believe you're free to do it, but to proceed without your
partner's say-so would "indulge the sinful nature" by ignoring your
responsibility to her. You are certainly free, for example, to spend
$500 for a new piece of furniture or that set of golf clubs you've had
your eye on, but to do so without consulting your spouse would be
to ignore mutual accountability.

Galatians 5:13 has something to say about balance in this area. A
paraphrase of this verse, applied to marriage, might read like this:
"Yes, you're free, but don't use your freedom to do your own thing,
apart from your spouse. Choose to serve your partner by respecting
her wishes as well. Love her by being accountable to her."

Accountability means realizing that your actions affect each
other. Webster's dictionary defines accountability this way:
"Obliged to account for one's acts." Marriage partners serve each
other by willingly laying aside their freedom to act alone. They
choose to account to each other for their acts.

If you're like most of us, you'll probably bump up against the
accountability issue in three areas of your marriage:

1. Your schedule. Do you have the right to make your own
schedule? Absolutely. If you're married, however, your schedule
affects your partner. In one of his films, James Dobson describes
coming home from a speaking engagement, anticipating a weekend of relaxing and watching college football. His wife, Shirley, on

the other hand, wanted him to do a few things around the house as well as spend some time with her. As a result of their differing expectations for the weekend, they argued. Couples can avoid such misunderstandings by being mutually accountable for their schedules and willing to communicate and negotiate with each other.

Ask yourselves these pertinent questions: Do we regularly coordinate our schedules? Do we communicate expectations for weekends? Do we consistently check with each other before inviting people to dinner or making other arrangements that affect us both? When we leave the house, do we tell each other where we're going and when we'll return?

2. Your money. No matter who earns the money in your family, you're both responsible for its use. If one of you often spends money without the other's approval, especially in large amounts, you'll run into problems. A wife told me recently that her husband bought a car without consulting her. She now had the pressure of the car payments on her shoulders. She was *not* happy!

Ask yourselves: Do we have a budget that we've both agreed to? Do we agree on how much we can spend without the other's approval? Do we pray about and talk through all major purchases? Do we listen to each other when we're concerned about finances?

3. Your parenting. Few activities affect the total function of a home as much as parenting. How you discipline your children and how you demonstrate love to them are key in bringing your family together. One common problem I've observed is that one parent tends to be authoritarian while the other tends to be permissive. But if you're accountable to each other, you can bring balance to this area.

Pertinent questions: Have we discussed our discipline philosophy and reached agreement about how to train our children? Do we consult with each other when confused about the appropriate course of action?

In the short run, it's easier to go your own way, exercising freedom as individuals without consulting each other. But if you allow yourselves to operate this way, you'll eventually run into problems. Instead, be accountable to each other. If you do, you'll enjoy the ultimate freedom of a healthy, happy relationship.

REFLECTIONS: Have you been accountable to each other with regard to your schedules, your money, and your parenting? If not, how can you submit to each other in these areas?

PRAYER FOCUS: Ask God to help you be responsible to each other in your marriage. Invite Him to show you how best to maintain accountability with each other.

111
WINNING THE
BATTLE OF WILLS

He who spares the rod hates his son, but he who loves
him is careful to discipline him.

PROVERBS 13:24

You've heard the radio and TV interviews, haven't you? You've heard the so-called experts say spanking is "hitting" and only teaches violence to a child. With so many voices promoting "communication-based" discipline, parents, especially new ones, may find themselves a bit confused. Even veteran parents can benefit from a timely exploration of the basics.

As I consider the topic of discipline, I believe we have a variety of valid resources to use. In my opinion, one of those resources, despite society's claims, is spanking. Why do I think parents need the disciplinary option of spanking their children? The following story provides a good explanation.

During his tenure as a practicing psychologist, James Dobson worked with a thirteen-year-old boy who was out of control. This young boy took drugs, wouldn't listen to his mother, and generally did his own thing.

Dobson asked his mother if she remembered when she first lost control of her son. She said that she knew exactly when it happened. When her son was three years old, she wanted him to lie down, so she put him in his crib. Instead, he stood up and spit in her face. She wiped off the spit and began explaining to him why spitting in her face was wrong. His response? He spit in her face again. She continued to talk to him until he spit in her face a third time. She was so flustered that she walked out of the room in confusion. "From that day forward," this woman explained, "I never had control again."[1]

At times, you won't be able to discipline your young children through communication alone. The Bible clearly explains why this is true. Psalm 51:5 tells us that every human being is "sinful at birth." Contrary to worldly wisdom that says we are all basically good, the Bible clearly indicates that human nature is bent by sin, that if left to ourselves we'll go the wrong way. Dobson's story vividly illustrates this truth. By nature, children will say, "I know what my parents want, but I'm going to do things my own way."

As parents, we need to set limits and enforce them, to make sure that our children *do not* get their own way because their own way will lead to their destruction. But as we do this, our kids will test our limits. Each child varies in how much he resists, but every child *will* resist. It's nonsense to believe that communication alone will win the battle of wills. Like the aforementioned mother with her three-year-old, parents will eventually face a discipline situation in which words aren't enough.

Proverbs 13:24 is pretty clear, isn't it? "He who spares the rod hates his son, but he who loves him is careful to discipline him." It seems evident to me that spanking is one of the tools at parents' disposal when disciplining their children. Yes, we need to use it wisely and correctly, with the child's good always in mind, but we must use it when necessary.

Or would you rather have your child continue to spit in your face?

REFLECTIONS: Whether or not you have children, do you agree about your disciplinary options? Do those options include spanking? Why or why not?

PRAYER FOCUS: Pray for your children, thanking God for them and asking for guidance to lovingly shape them through appropriate discipline.

112
HOW TO SPANK
YOUR CHILD

The rod of correction imparts wisdom,
but a child left to himself disgraces his mother.
PROVERBS 29:15

Do you both agree about how and when to spank your children, or has inconsistency dogged your parenting style? While Scriptures indicate that parents should use corporal punishment when necessary—the image of the "rod of correction" is fairly clear—they don't offer many details beyond that. At some point, you'll have to make these decisions for yourselves. So how can you wisely and consistently fill in the details of Proverbs 29:15?

One couple told me they hadn't thought much about discipline until their daughter turned three. At that point, it seemed like a "self-will switch" was thrown somewhere deep in this little girl's heart. When told to pick up her toys, she would say, "No!" If she resisted further, her parents would give her a "time out" (three minutes in a neutral corner). But often this strategy wasn't effective. The little girl wouldn't stay in her corner or cooperate with the process. So what began as a simple request for her to pick up her toys escalated time and again. Self-will was out in force!

These parents wanted to teach their little girl wisdom but needed to know when and how to spank her. My counsel to them was simple: Use spanking in response to deliberate acts of disobedience. When a child thumbs her nose at your authority, bring out the heavy artillery. So, for example, you should not spank your child if she accidentally spills her milk. In a case like this, she hasn't deliberately rejected your parental authority. However, if she runs away from you when you call, you may spank her because she has deliberately challenged your authority. If you can't decide whether your child has deliberately disobeyed you, I recommend erring on the side of leniency: Choose not to spank this time, but communicate clearly for next time.

You need to decide not only when to spank but also how. I strongly believe that parents should spank their children on the fleshy part of the bottom, nowhere else. Spanking this area produces some pain, but no damage. And a child usually needs no more than a few swats. Some parents prefer to spank with a neutral object, such as a wooden spoon, rather than their hands. Others find such paddles offensive and prefer to swat with their hands.

When possible, I suggest making the spanking an "event." Before you spank your child, ask her, "Honey, why am I spanking you? What did you do wrong?" Remember that spanking is designed to develop wisdom. Asking your child if she understands the reasons for the spanking helps her take responsibility for her actions. If your child doesn't understand why you're spanking her, the spanking loses its purpose.

When you feel certain that your child knows why she is being spanked, ask her to bend over and give her the swats. Afterward, hold your child and reassure her of your love. I realize that children sometimes do not cooperate in this process, but it's best to have a strategy even if you can't always follow it.

Sometime soon your little one will likely challenge your authority. Isn't it about time to determine a clear and consistent response? Ask God for clarity and guidance as you "impart wisdom" to your precious children.

REFLECTIONS: In what areas are you battling your children right now? Is spanking appropriate at these times, or should you employ some other method of discipline? Do you agree about how and when to spank your children?

PRAYER FOCUS: Ask God to give you clear insight each day into when your children need spanking and how to do it appropriately. Pray for God's wisdom as parents.

113
BUILDING WISDOM IN YOUR CHILDREN

Love the LORD your God with all your heart and
with all your soul and with all your strength. These commandments
that I give you today are to be upon your hearts. Impress them on your
children. Talk about them when you sit at home and when you walk
along the road, when you lie down and when you get up.

DEUTERONOMY 6:5–7

Having listened to many parents over the years, I think most parents feel inadequate about fulfilling their spiritual responsibilities to their children; in fact, they feel more inadequate in this area than in any other. They feel pressure to do family devotions and to consistently share Bible times with their children, but they just can't seem to pull it off as they'd like. Many parents constantly feel a low level of guilt concerning what they *aren't* doing spiritually.

Helping your children see life from God's perspective is a challenging and sometimes elusive task. Yet the fact remains that parents not only need to drive foolishness *out,* they also need to build godly wisdom *in.* Deuteronomy 6:5–7 has some good news for parents struggling with this responsibility. It suggests a method for building God's values, perspective, and character into your children's lives. You might be surprised at how simple, and above all, how doable this method really is.

How do you build godly wisdom into your children's lives? It begins with your godly *example,* loving "the LORD your God with all your heart and with all your soul and with all your strength." The first and perhaps best way for parents to form godly character in their children is to model it themselves. Watching his parent love God day in and day out can't help but make an indelible impression on a child's mind and heart. Your children will watch you when an unexpected bill arrives or when someone cuts you off in traffic. They'll observe you as you make a difficult decision or unravel a thorny problem. And you'll impress God's values on your children as you live out His values in the schoolroom of life.

You also build wisdom in your children through *informal teaching*. This is teaching that occurs as "you walk along the road." All parents know about those teachable moments in life when a child is ripe for listening to God's point of view. In the course of everyday life, situations inevitably arise that raise questions in a child's mind. What a great time to talk informally, bringing God's perspective into the discussion. Not too long ago, my family was eating lunch when my youngest daughter, Sarah, asked this question: "Mom, how are Mormons different from Christians?" We spent a few profitable moments talking about the doctrine of salvation and the person of Jesus. How's that for a teachable moment?

Finally, there's a place for *formal teaching* times with your children. "Talk about them when you sit at home..." implies planning and intentionality. Since every family is different, this concept will vary a good deal in its application. Young families might profit from reading a Bible storybook and answering simple discussion questions together. Other families might want to read a Bible passage at dinnertime and discuss its implications. Parents need to be creative, understanding what their children might best respond to. For example, during my children's fifth- and sixth-grade years, I've made it a point to join each one of them for daily quiet times, teaching them how to pray and read God's Word. We all enjoyed those times together—and learned a lot, too!

You can be flexible as you build wisdom in your children. Just make sure that you *are* doing it, impressing on your children a love for God that takes all their heart, soul, and strength.

REFLECTIONS: Think about the three methods for building wisdom in your children. How can you apply each element to help your children learn to love God?

PRAYER FOCUS: Take some time to ask God for specific insight into the many parenting challenges you face. Ask Him to open your eyes to opportunities for instilling love for Him in your children.

114
THE MAKER OF
HEAVEN AND EARTH

My help comes from the LORD, the Maker of heaven and earth.
PSALM 121:2

Need some help? Wondering how things will turn out in your marriage or family? Do solutions seem far away?

Consider where your help comes from: "the Maker of heaven and earth." If your Maker can create all of heaven and earth, can't He create a solution for your difficulties? To fully grasp His abilities, pause for a moment and put your problems in perspective as you wonder at His creation.

On a family visit to Olympic National Park several years ago, we stopped by "The Grove of the Patriarchs," a small stand of two-thousand-year-old Douglas fir trees. As we walked through that forest and stood beside the massive trunks of those trees, I was dwarfed by their sheer dimensions and overcome by their beauty. The One who created such beauty—He's where your help comes from!

Think about the human body. The human eye alone is so sophisticated that scientists still don't completely understand how it works. Packed with automatic aiming, focusing, and aperture adjustment, it makes 100,000 separate movements every day. It sends a constant stream of color pictures to the brain that are truly amazing.[1] And the human eye is only one feature of the human body, all designed by God, our Maker. The One who designed and created the incredibly complex systems of human life—He's where your help comes from!

Now imagine the intricacies of this planet we live on. Think of how God has created this earth to exact specifications. Consider these facts from science:

• If the earth rotated just one-tenth slower or faster than its present rate, no plant life could exist on the earth because of the resulting temperature variations.

• If the moon were located one-fifth closer to the earth, all land would be completely covered by water twice a day because of massive tides.

• If the earth's crust and the depth of its oceans were increased only a few feet, plant life couldn't exist because the absorption of free oxygen and carbon dioxide would be drastically altered.[2]

The Maker of planet Earth—He's where your help comes from!

Go even further with me, if you will. This earth and all the life it contains only hint at our Maker's infinite power. Think of the awesome complexity and scope of the universe in which we live. According to astronomers, you'd have to travel at the speed of light for four years to arrive at the closet star outside our solar system, yet you'd reach only one star within one solar system. Scientists tell us that millions upon millions of stars exist, contained within thousands of galaxies. And all these stars, planets, solar systems, and galaxies are apparently in perpetual motion, thoughtfully designed and managed to work in synchronized perfection.

Now pause for a moment and remember the Source of your help. The One who promises to help you is the Maker of heaven and earth. If He has created each of us, the world we live in, and the universe in which we exist, do you think your problems are too big for Him to handle?

I don't know about you, but when I consider the awesome capabilities of the Maker of heaven and earth and remember that my help comes from Him, somehow my problems don't seem so large.

PRAYER FOCUS: No discussion today. As you wonder at God's creation, give Him praise and thanks for all He has made. Then ask the Maker of heaven and earth for whatever help you need.

115
AN ETERNAL
PERSPECTIVE

Therefore we do not lose heart.... For our light and momentary
troubles are achieving for us an eternal glory that far outweighs them
all. So we fix our eyes not on what is seen, but on what is unseen.
For what is seen is temporary, but what is unseen is eternal.

2 CORINTHIANS 4:16–18

If we want to go through life with a positive attitude, what we need
most is an eternal perspective. In fact, to maintain balance in our
marriages and families in this imperfect world, an eternal perspective is essential.

What's an eternal perspective? "Perspective" can mean one's
point of view, vantage point, outlook, or frame of reference. Your
perspective is essentially your way of looking at events and attach-
ing meaning to them. Think of the difference between looking
through a camera with a micro-lens (the kind designed to take
close-ups of objects very near at hand) and the perspective gained
with a wide-angle lens capable of taking in whole mountain
ranges. Quite a difference in perspective, isn't it? The lens you look
through affects what you see and how you see it.

An eternal perspective, then, means looking at life through the
wide-angle lens of eternity.

Perspective is really important. How you view the world affects
how you approach life's challenges. You can view life's experiences
in two ways: from a temporary viewpoint or from an eternal one.
Either you can see life's events as having meaning for this world
alone—in which case negative or disappointing events appear ran-
dom and void of meaning—or you can choose to see them in the
context of eternity. The former leads ultimately to depression, anxiety, and hopelessness; the latter, to joy, hope, and security.

Paul says that life's troubles have eternal significance. In fact, he says that these trials can potentially achieve "eternal glory" in your life. Simply put, difficulties produce character. As you weather the pain of a problem, you can potentially grow closer to God and develop a more Christlike character. That's why Paul could say that his rather prodigious difficulties were "light and momentary troubles."

Couples who fix their eyes on the unseen reality of God Himself walk through this world with joy, finding God's best through each difficulty. I could name couple after couple who have taken an eternal perspective. One couple has a retarded son; another struggles through the wife's multiple sclerosis; a third has faced the uncertainty of three layoffs in the last two years; yet another has struggled for years under an unfair IRS bill that has crippled the family's finances. I could go on and on. How do these couples make it through life? They fix their eyes on the eternal. They maintain perspective.

Am I taking a cavalier attitude toward people's problems? Not at all. I understand (and have felt) the pain that life can sometimes inflict, but the Bible is clear: *Your problems are not as important as your perspective.*

You may be looking at a set of problems right now that look anything but small. In fact, you may have an ongoing difficulty that looks as if it will never end. Let me encourage you to adopt an eternal perspective. You can look toward God, growing through the difficulty as you trust in Him. In Him, you can find a place of peace and joy. What does it take? Putting on that wide-angle lens of eternity and seeing from God's perspective.

REFLECTIONS: Have you found it difficult to view your problems with an eternal perspective? Do you face one of those problems right now? What will it take to look at that challenge with eternity in mind?

PRAYER FOCUS: Ask God to give you His perspective on any difficulties you currently face.

116
BELIEVE IN EACH OTHER

I have great confidence in you; I take great pride in you.
2 CORINTHIANS 7:4

Remember when you were new on the job, wondering if you could succeed? Or how about the time you took on that new ministry at church and felt inadequate to fulfill the call?

At times like those you probably needed one thing more than any other: someone to believe in you, someone to say, "You can do it. I'm behind you. I have confidence in you."

And in those challenging undertakings, who provided those words of encouragement? Most likely, your marriage partner stood right behind you, just as it should be. Spouses need to be each other's number-one cheerleader in life. For a good model of this, just look at Paul's words of encouragement to the Corinthian believers. When your partner puts it on the line, stretching her wings, she needs to know that you have confidence in her. When she's given her best, she needs to know that you're proud of her.

Most of us tend to doubt ourselves and our abilities from time to time. When our belief in ourselves wanes, a partner who says, "I have confidence in you," spurs us forward, releasing us to do our best. Each of us desperately longs to hear the words "I know you can do it." Those simple words can make all the difference.

I was amused some time ago to hear of a mayor and his wife who were walking along a city street. As they rounded a corner, they noticed a construction worker busy on the street. Looking more closely, the mayor recognized this man as his wife's former fiancé.

In fun, the mayor quipped, "Look, if you had married him, you'd now be the wife of a construction worker."

She retorted, "If I had married him, he'd now be the mayor of this city."

Who knows? She may have been right. When you believe in each other, you help each other achieve goals you wouldn't have reached otherwise. If you listen to great people talk about themselves, they will often mention their spouses' influence. Billy Graham has said of his wife, Ruth, "She has been vital to my life and an integral part our ministry."[1] I'm positive that Ruth's belief in her husband has significantly contributed to his accomplishments.

Without Naomi's confidence in my abilities and her constant support, I have no doubt that I would have accomplished less and given up more often. Through a college degree and two graduate degrees, through the challenge of various ministry assignments, through the writing of several books, her support has kept me going when I wanted to quit. When I've found it hard to believe in myself, her belief has spurred me on.

Want to give each other a gift no one else can give? Want to infuse each other's heart with new strength? Believe in each other!

REFLECTIONS: Tell your spouse about a time in the past when his or her confidence in you has meant the most. Now tell your partner how you need support right now. Finish by expressing pride in one of your partner's recent accomplishments.

PRAYER FOCUS: Thank God for your spouse, specifically for your partner's positive traits. Now ask your spouse how you can pray specifically for him or her.

117
THE KEY TO A
CHILD'S OBEDIENCE

*Now the overseer... must manage his own family well and see
that his children obey him with proper respect.*

1 TIMOTHY 3:2, 4

What about it, parents? Do you manage your household well? Do
your children obey you? Are harmony and order present in your
home?

Tough questions, I know. I do think, however, that most
Christian parents would answer yes. But why?

I believe 1 Timothy 3 provides a good part of the answer. You
can sum it up in one word: respect. Obedience is linked to respect.
When children respect their parents, they tend to mind them. It's
that simple. When you foster respect, your children will respond to
your leadership. Oh, you can demand certain behavior from
younger children, but teenagers will obey you only if they respect
you, and you have to earn that respect when your kids are young.

A number of troubled families have come to me for counseling
over the years. My heart has ached to see these households in disar-
ray. Again and again, I've watched disrespectful children virtually
paralyze families. Sometimes a family's problem has boiled down
to one rebellious child, and in most of these cases, the child's lack of
respect was a direct result of parental actions.

So how do parents earn their children's respect? Two
absolutely necessary behaviors come to mind. First, parents must
build good relationships with their children. Leadership without
relationship will fail. This can be an especially tricky issue for parents who work outside the home. A career can siphon off your
energy and leave little time for developing relationships with your
children. Moms and dads must ask themselves, "How much

energy are we leaving for the home front?"

If you don't take the time and energy to build relationships with your children, your efforts at leadership will only produce resentment. However, when you take the time to stay in contact with your kids and give them your ongoing, focused attention, they'll respond to you on all levels. And when you build relationships with your kids, you foster the respect necessary for effective discipline.

Parents also earn respect by *fostering consistency*. This relates primarily to character. When children see that a parent's behavior matches his words, they respect him. This principle is global, applying to almost everything in a parent's life. Consistent parents set limits with their children, then enforce them. Consistent parents make promises, then keep their word. Consistent parents treat each child with love and don't show favoritism. I'm not talking about perfection here—kids understand mistakes—but you do need to "walk your talk" in all areas of life. As you do, your children's respect for you will grow.

And as their respect deepens, they'll become more likely to do what you ask of them.

Do you sense tension between you and your kids right now? If so, develop relationships and consistency with your children. As you do, you'll encourage harmony and order in your home.

REFLECTIONS: Evaluate your relationships with your children and the consistency of your actions. What are you doing well? What could you improve? Gently discuss changes you might need to make.

PRAYER FOCUS: Pray for God to give you insight about and empowerment for parenting. Ask Him to help you foster respect with your children through relationships and consistency.

118
GENUINE LOVE
STANDS OUT

*Jesus replied: "'Love the Lord your God with all your heart and
with all your soul and with all your mind.' This is the first
and greatest commandment. And the second is like it: 'Love
your neighbor as yourself.' All the Law and the Prophets
hang on these two commandments."*

MATTHEW 22:37–40

During my college years in the early '70s, a man named Bill Nolan
started attending our little Baptist church. Only thirty-eight years
old, Bill was a lieutenant colonel in the army. Having completed
two tours in Vietnam, he was stationed in Bellevue, Washington,
for the coming three years.

I'll never forget him.

I was only twenty years old at the time, but I knew Bill pos-
sessed something very rare. He was the real thing, what a genuine
Christian should be. From the moment he started attending our
church, he began to demonstrate his love for God by ministering to
others. Never showy, certainly never pushy, Bill just got out there
and did what needed doing.

I remember the pastor mentioning one Sunday that the church
building needed painting. Without any fanfare, Bill spent three
days painting and finished the entire church by the next weekend.
He never told anyone and certainly didn't expect any praise. Bill
painted that church as an act of love for our busy pastor, and I still
remember the smile on our pastor's face the next Sunday.

Bill also started a Bible study for some of us young college and
career folks. It was a small group, and looking back, I realize that
Bill didn't have a great deal in common with us. Yet he was there
for us every week, demonstrating love in concrete ways. Bill was

always available to talk, to help, to pray, or even to play a game or two. A balanced person, he was always a lot of fun.

But it was his love for God that stood out. Bill actually lived out his faith. He knew what it meant to love God and others.

Just before I graduated from the University of Washington, Bill told me he had an important decision to make. As an army officer, he had been stationed in Korea for a time, and had begun to minister to the street kids of Seoul, South Korea. He never forgot the desperate plight of those kids. Now he faced a decision. Should he stay in the army and possibly receive a promotion to general someday, or should he retire to Seoul and minister to street kids on his retirement pay?

Knowing Bill, I shouldn't have been surprised that he chose to retire and move to Seoul. In the years since, he has lived in Korea, taking kids into his own home, educating them, feeding them, and leading them to Christ. Twenty years later, scores of kids have been blessed by Bill's genuine love for God.

I'll never forget Bill, a man who lived out Jesus' great commandment to love God and to love others. I never heard Bill brag about himself or lift himself up as an example. He didn't have to. Genuine love stands out.

REFLECTIONS: Has anyone ever impressed you as a person who genuinely loves God and others? How did that person's genuine love impact you and others? How can you seek to fulfill Jesus' great commandment in your life?

PRAYER FOCUS: Ask God to help you live out your love for Him and for others in concrete ways that make a difference.

119
A 10 PERCENT GAIN

Finally, brothers, we instructed you how to live in order to please
God.... Now we ask you...to do this more and more.

1 THESSALONIANS 4:1

Think what would happen in your marriage this year if you experienced a 10 percent improvement in one or two key areas of your relationship, such as spending time together or resolving your conflicts. Think what would happen if you continued that improvement year after year, finding greater and greater satisfaction in your relationship together. Such growth would thoroughly revolutionize your marriage.

Paul's encouragement to the Thessalonians reveals a key principle for all believers which applies to the marriage relationship: The Christian walk is a process that *gradually* transforms one's character. In essence, Paul says, "Believers are to please God, and they are to do so *more and more.*" Continual and gradual change is God's plan for our lives.

This principle offers great encouragement to married couples. Growth in a couple's relationship, like all spiritual growth, is gradual. A husband and wife wanting to grow think about key areas of need, then cooperate with each other and with God for gradual change. Their relationship reflects this and grows through persistent effort over time.

Viewing change this way can keep you from becoming overwhelmed. After all, some changes take years. For example, a husband and wife might believe they need to handle conflict better but feel overwhelmed by the task. However, if they agree that they can improve 10 percent in their conflict-resolution skills, suddenly they have a doable goal. With God's help, any couple can please

Him in their marriage relationship "more and more."

It's tempting to give up, thinking change is just too hard. Even more detrimental to the change process is the attitude "That's just the way I am; I can't change it." Such an attitude will cause your marriage to atrophy. Growth in your relationship will grind to a halt. Not only that, such an attitude directly defies Paul's call to please God more and more.

This concept can be difficult to comprehend for people who think in black and white. Years ago, I worked with a couple in which the husband could not accept gradual change. He had an "all or nothing" attitude. He wanted change, and he wanted it *now*. If he could have accepted a 10 percent change as a good start, his marriage would have grown immeasurably. As it was, he often felt like giving up on himself and his spouse.

Couples need to discuss small ways in which they can change and then patiently work together to make these changes happen. Total turnabouts rarely occur, but 10 percent improvements can have a tremendous impact. Think what positive changes the 10 percent rule could bring to your marriage. You'll talk 10 percent more, go on 10 percent more dates, resolve conflict 10 percent more effectively, or demonstrate caring behaviors 10 percent more.

Come on. You can do it! Work together to nurture your marriage "more and more." See what a difference a 10 percent improvement can make.

REFLECTIONS: What areas of your marriage could benefit from growth? Which area would you most like to work on? How can you make a 10 percent change in that area? Are you both willing to commit to working on your relationship in that way?

PRAYER FOCUS: Ask God to help you change more and more in the area(s) you've identified.

120
LOVE IS EVERYTHING
YOUR FAMILY NEEDS

*Therefore, as God's chosen people, holy and dearly loved, clothe
yourselves with compassion, kindness, humility, gentleness
and patience.... And over all these virtues put on love,
which binds them all together in perfect unity.*

COLOSSIANS 3:12, 14

We all have a lot to learn about being effective fathers and mothers, husbands and wives. In fact, there's so much to learn that couples often feel overwhelmed. Have you been there? Do you sometimes feel that you're not doing enough, that everyone else probably does it better? Do you cringe at your own failures and wonder if you're really doing the job?

Let me simplify family life for you: "Put on love." There it is. Love is everything your family needs. It binds all virtues into one and covers your family with a warm blanket of security. Your love, expressed daily, is the best gift you can give to your family and especially to each other.

My son Jon is in junior high school this year, a tough age for any boy, and I sometimes feel I'm not as good a father as I could be. I haven't gone fishing or played catch with him in a while. I don't live up to the perfect-father stereotype wedged firmly in my mind. But I do enfold Jon in love. I'm gentle and kind to him. I speak words of encouragement to him. Love comes his way every day, whether I'm able to give him full, personal attention that day or not.

Certainly, our children need time with us, and they need our guidance. They need wise fathers and mothers. But genuine love expressed daily will make up for almost any inadequacy. Jon said something recently that proves it. Every day before Jon goes to

school, he and I have a quiet time together. We both value that
focused attention. As we prayed together one morning not long ago,
Jon prayed, "Lord, I'm thankful for my dad. Thank you that he
loves me just the way I am and that he's always kind to me."

Love is everything your family needs.

That's true in your marriage relationship as well. You understand that your partner makes mistakes. You understand that he
sometimes ignores the budget, that she sometimes makes you late.
You understand that you both live with imperfect people. But when
you offer self-giving love on a regular basis, imperfections are over-
looked. The gifts of compassion, kindness, humility, gentleness, and
patience, all wrapped in the brightly colored paper of love, will do
more to sustain your relationship than anything else.

I have two friends who have been married to each other for
some time. The husband has a fault which hurts his wife a great
deal: He is driven in his profession. He regularly puts in long hours
at the office. And because he doesn't set his boundaries very well, his
colleagues tend to treat him unfairly and give him even more work.
To some degree, he has sacrificed family time to win approval from
his fellow workers. This couple has communicated about the problem and worked on it for years. Periodically they see some
improvement, but the basic problem stills exists.

This problem might have brought some marriages to the brink
of divorce. This couple, however, remains close. Their relationship
has survived this problem. How? This husband and wife exhibit
love. Daily, they exchange expressions of love with each other. Kind
words, caring acts, and patient love are the norm. Everything else is
simply less important.

We all want to be the best parents and the best marriage partners we can be. And we should do what we can to pursue excellence
in our family relationships. But always remember, especially when
you feel inadequate, that love is everything your family needs.

REFLECTIONS: Affirm each other. Tell about the concrete ways you see each other express love to your family.

PRAYER FOCUS: Pray for a fresh infusion of love and for ways to practically express it to your children and to each other.

NOTES

Introduction
1. James Dobson, *Love for a Lifetime* (Sisters, Ore.: Multnomah Books, 1987), 50.

Devotion 8
1. Mike Mason, *The Mystery of Marriage* (Sisters, Ore.: Multnomah Press, 1983), 55–56.

Devotion 11
1. Robert A. Bork, *Sloughing Towards Gomorrah* (New York: HarperCollins Publishers, Inc., 1996), 21.

Devotion 15
1. Mike Mason, *The Mystery of Marriage* (Sisters, Ore.: Multnomah Press, 1983), 83.

Devotion 30
1. C. S. Lewis, *Mere Christianity* (New York: Macmillan Publishing Company, 1952), 77, 86.

Devotion 33
1. Robert Fulghum, "Sigmund Wollman's Reality Test," *Readers Digest*, December 1993, 52.

Devotion 41
1. C. S. Lewis, *The Silver Chair* (New York: Macmillan Publishing Company, 1953), 146.

Devotion 46
1. Henry Cloud, *Changes That Heal* (Grand Rapids, Mich.: Zondervan Publishing House, 1990), 46.

Devotion 52
1. Mike Mason, *The Mystery of Marriage* (Sisters, Ore.: Multnomah Press, 1985), 65–66.

Devotion 53
1. Neil Warren, *The Triumphant Marriage* (Colorado Springs, Colo.: Focus on the Family, 1995), 31.

Devotion 57
1. Steven R. Covey, *The Seven Habits of Highly Effective People* (New York: Simon & Schuster, 1989), 241.

Devotion 61
1. Ted Engstrom, *A Time for Commitment* (Grand Rapids, Mich.: Zondervan Publishing House, 1987), 86–87.

Devotion 70
1. Alan Loy McGinnis, *The Friendship Factor* (Minneapolis, Minn.: Augsburg Publishing House, 1979), 110.

Devotion 74
1. C. S. Lewis, *Letters to Malcolm: Chiefly on Prayer* (London: Geoffrey Bles, 1964), 26–27.

Devotion 85
1. Ed Wheat and Gaye Wheat, *Intended for Pleasure* (Old Tappen, N.J.: Flemming H. Revell Company, 1981), 16.

Devotion 103
1. Paul Stevens, *Marriage Spirituality* (Downers Grove, Ill.: InterVarsity Press, 1989), 128.

Devotion 104
1. Alan Loy McGinnis, *The Friendship Factor* (Minneapolis, Minn.: Augsburg Publishing House, 1979), 123.

Devotion 107

1. "The 1990 Virginia Slims Opinion Poll," conducted by the Roper Organization, Inc., Roper Center, University of Connecticut, Storrs, Connecticut 06268.

2. James Dobson, *Love for a Lifetime* (Sisters, Ore.: Multnomah Books, 1993), 58.

Devotion 111

1. James Dobson, *Focus on the Family* radio broadcast, May 22, 1997.

Devotion 114

1. Scott M. Huse, *The Collapse of Evolution* (Grand Rapids, Mich.: Baker Books, 1993), 92.

2. Huse, 71–72.

Devotion 116

1. Billy Graham, *Just As I Am* (New York: HarperCollins Publishers, 1997), 735.